MORNINGSTAR

MORNINGSTAR
A WARRIOR'S SPIRIT

MORNINGSTAR MERCREDI

COTEAU BOOKS

Edited by Roberta Coulter.
Cover portrait: "Morningstar Mercredi," by Greg Huszar, Greg Huszar Photography
Cover and book design by Duncan Campbell.
Printed and bound in Canada by Marquis Bookprinting Inc.

Library and Archives Canada Cataloguing in Publication

Mercredi, Morningstar
      Morningstar : a warrior's spirit / Morningstar Mercredi.

ISBN 1-55050-346-4

1. Mercredi, Morningstar.   2. Tinne women—Biography.
3. Recovering addicts—Canada, Northern—Biography.
4. Sexual abuse victims—Canada, Northern—Biography. I. Title.

E99.T56M47 2006   362.83'089972   C2006-903594-6

10 9 8 7 6 5 4 3

2517 Victoria Avenue
Regina, Saskatchewan
Canada S4P 0T2

Available in Canada & the US from
Fitzhenry & Whiteside
195 Allstate Parkway
Markham, ON, Canada L3R 4T8

The publisher gratefully acknowledges the financial assistance of the Saskatchewan Arts Board, the Canada Council for the Arts, the Government of Canada through the Book Publishing Industry Development Program (BPIDIP), the Association for the Export of Canadian Books, the Government of Saskatchewan, through the Cultural Industries Development Fund, and the City of Regina Arts Commission, for its publishing program.

*In loving memory
of Dwayne Desjarlais*

*In spirit and in loving memory
of Brenda Gilchrist*

INTRODUCTION

From the darkness came the first light between Father Sky and Mother Earth, and then there was light, the sun – the beginning of life. On the first dawn, a star shone before the sun, the morning star. This eastern star represents illumination and guidance, the destiny between the Star Nation and Mother Earth.

I'm assured that long after I take my last breath, the earth will orbit in this galaxy. And just as sure as the sun appears to rise, it sets elsewhere on earth, and then Grandmother Moon stirs currents, instigating change through her lunar presence.

There are as many people who will relate to my story as there are visible stars in the galaxy. Some of those stars no longer exist, but we still see them on a clear night. They remain in hindsight. Their image and impact remain throughout generations.

In the tapestry of creation, each thread is interwoven with all the others. The beauty of each thread connects to the whole. Should any one be ignored, the greater picture is skewed. Should any one be broken or frayed, the whole fabric is blemished.

My name is Morningstar; my spirit name is Wandering Earth Spirit Woman. I did not ask for these names, and I was deeply humbled when I received them. Since then, I have come to understand that the spirit works anonymously and is all-knowing. How could I have known my life would be defined by my name Morningstar, or that I would live my life according to my spirit name? How could I have known then that Morningstar would purge the pain of my past, nurturing change and growth within me?

My story springs from changes imposed by a foreign government and foreign religions affecting every Aboriginal person in Canada. Imagine, if you can, a stranger coming to your door to take your children when they are only four or five years old. They are kept from you until they are grown. You see them only seasonally, for visits. There is nothing you can do but watch and wait. They are taught to speak in a foreign language. They are abused, neglected and numbered.

Think the unthinkable. Your children are molested, denied affection, malnourished and silenced.

Do these thoughts anger you, enrage you? What would you do? What if you could do nothing? You are powerless over a government that has legally oppressed you and denied you your children.

Residential schools institutionalized generations of Aboriginal children. So many people say, "It's the past – let it go. Forget about it." Would these wounds be so easy to forget, to mend? How long would it take to break you, to numb you? How long would it take before you surrendered your fight for your children? Would you give up? Forget about it?

It took four generations for Aboriginal people to win the right to raise their own children. And this fight wasn't over even after the last residential school was closed in the mid 1970s, the last of 130 institutions that were opened in the mid 1860s. We still live with the aftermath of beating the Indian out of generations of Aboriginal children. What happens over four generations? Maybe all that was left was the will to survive, to exist through generations of genocide and oppression, until hope became as elusive as prayer.

In my family, there are three generations of survivors of residential schools. When my mom was released, her experience was passed onto me. I am a survivor of intergenerational impact of residential schools. This impact is systemic and far too deep and severe to ignore. We are only now discovering the implications of this part of Canadian history. In many ways, we are still reeling from this burden.

Yet there is a quiet calm. I can feel it, see it. Spirit is manifesting change. I know the spirit of Aboriginal people is not broken. I have shared our history with my son. I did not deny him the truth. I saw the pain in his eyes, but I see strength in him too.

Together we have begun to mend generational wounds. Our sacred fire is strong and our spirit intact. We remain children of Mother Earth and Father Sky. This is the story of many, and with as much humanity and compassion as the Great Mystery grants me, let me share with you *our* story.

Let us mend our star blankets, step out of ignorance and denial to a place where we, as a human race, can understand each other's pain. Let us respect the sound of truth reverberating in the universe and hear those cries once silenced.

I am Morningstar, and this is a warrior's spirit.

GYPSY SPIRIT

She runs across the street, startled like a coyote in the oncoming headlights. Pebbles hurt her bare feet, but she doesn't notice the pain. Buses, cars and people pass. Some of them glance at her only briefly with curiosity, while others stop for a moment and stare as a five-year-old girl in pyjamas panics past them. Their stares unnerve her. Buildings tower over her while sirens scream past and several vehicles honk their horns; the noise chases her. The chill of the cold autumn wind clings to her bare skin beneath her pyjamas and makes her catch her breath. She knows where she has to go. She remains fixed on her destination, knowing her sisters are locked in the basement suite with the babysitter. Impatiently waiting for another red light to turn green, she ignores the anxiety building in her as she watches the busy traffic. Her will is greater than fear.

Mom had been away a long time, and I didn't know when she was coming home. She'd left a babysitter to take care of us six girls. The oldest of us was seven, the baby a couple months old. I was five.

We were scared of the babysitter. He hurt us when he touched us, making my sisters cry. We locked ourselves in Mom's bedroom and pushed the dresser against the door. I decided to get Mom. My sisters helped me crawl out the window of our basement suite. I escaped barefoot in my flannel pyjamas.

I had no coat, but fear of the babysitter made my body feel more numb than the cold air. I began the long walk up Jasper Avenue to the Cecil Hotel. That's where Mom usually went when she went out. My feet grew chilled as I marched along the cement sidewalks and crossed the streets, dodging the busy traffic as I ran across the roads. I had urgency in my steps.

I knew that if I stayed on Jasper Avenue I would eventually reach the Cecil Hotel. I remembered the way from the bus rides along Jasper when Mom took us with her, then made us wait in the restaurant while she went into the bar.

Twenty-one blocks later, I found the hotel. I pulled the heavy doors open and asked the man behind the desk to page my mom, Ann McCarty.

When she came out of the bar, she was drunk. I asked, "Mommy will you come home now?" She was taken aback to see me.

"How the hell did you get here?" she said, looking around to see if anyone was with me.

"I walked. Will you come home now?" I pleaded.

She told me to wait for her, then staggered back into the bar, returning in a few moments with cases of beer and several strangers. We all jumped into a taxi and went home.

They carried on partying, and she didn't get angry at me for finding her.

In order to survive, I had to deny what happened. Minimizing emotions and denying traumatic events are methods of survival. Even now, I want to believe my childhood wasn't that bad, that there were good times. And there were, but denying or smothering my voice suffocates the child who fought to stay alive, and every child has a right to their voice; every child deserves a life beyond silence and secrets; every warrior needs to be honoured...

My parents married young: Lawrence and Ann McCarty. Their first-born was a boy. Mom's relations warned her not to spend too much time with her grandmother, who was ill and would die soon and might take the baby with her on her spirit journey. After her grandmother passed away, Mom gave birth to my brother. He was stillborn. Her grandmother had taken my brother with her to spirit world. I believe this – I have no reason not to. Others say Mom worked too hard taking care of her grandmother while she was pregnant. Either way, my brother didn't live.

Mom went on to have seven daughters. I'm the second oldest. Mom named me Jolene Mavis McCarty. I was born in a northern mining town, Uranium City, Saskatchewan, but Fort Chipewyan in Alberta has always been home. My ancestors settled there during the fur-trade era. I don't know if it's the town that is home so much as the land and Lake Athabasca.

My Native grandmothers gave me my black-brown hair, dark-brown eyes, and spunky spirit. Although I wish I had the light eyes of Dad's Scottish or Irish grandfathers, I know I have their hot-blooded temperament.

I can only imagine the strong chemistry that was ignited when my voyaging grandfathers met my Native grandmothers. Both sides were strong willed survivors in their own right. My ancestors' nomadic nature cultivated a legacy over generations. Their gypsy spirit is in my blood.

Dad's grandmothers, on both sides of his family, were Native women whose lives contributed significantly in the establishment of Rupert's Land, although the Native wives of the Scottish, Irish and French traders have only started to be given due respect by historians. It was inevitable that men would need the comfort of women, but I doubt any of these voyaging forefathers fully appreciated how much their survival depended upon Aboriginal women as they settled in this vast wild land. It has always been common knowledge in our communities that the women are the strength of the people.

In my family, the mothers of the Métis were Chipewyan, Cree, Anishinabe, and I'm told, Mi'kmaq. Our bloodline flows like the rivers and streams they portaged when opening Canada's frontier. Families were established along the shores as our grandfathers and grandmothers lived, loved and left their legacy on the land for generations to follow. It's safe to say that the women grounded these men firmly in this New World.

It's difficult to imagine how beaver pelts, lynx, wolf and several four-legged critters created the current-in-sea that brought the Europeans over the ocean to this New World, a world filled with folklore and fantasy of the original inhabitants.

My lineage is Irish, Scottish and French too. I'm told that some of my ancestors are buried in Montreal. All I know for certain is that my Scottish ancestors arrived a few hundred years ago on the east coast, from which they dispersed, and my great grandfather made his way west with his brother. They may have been kicked out of their own land; perhaps the promise of wealth and prosperity through the fur trade in this New World enticed them to leave their land, or maybe they were seeking freedom from repression in Scotland. Nonetheless, I do know that when they arrived here, the French priests changed our original Scottish name to a French surname.

It appears the genes of my grandmothers were stronger than those of the Europeans, and the result is dark skin and striking features in my family. In Dad's youth, he looked like a halfbreed James Dean in his black leather jacket. He rolled up the cuffs of his jeans and wore a T-shirt beneath his dress shirt. He walked proudly, heightening his six-foot-two frame and squaring his broad shoulders. Handsome and suave-looking, he greased his dark brown hair back, combed to one side. He looked cool, but his mischievous brown eyes always gave him away.

Dad had his own band as a young man, and like his father, he played the fiddle. He sang all the old country greats of the 1950s, Hank Williams Sr. and such, or he'd get the crowd jigging and square dancing. He was smooth, smooth enough to catch and keep the attention of Mom for many years.

Mom's parents were predominantly Chipewyan and part French. Mom's high cheekbones and chiselled features displayed her Indian ancestry. She was a northern beauty with sultry dark brown eyes, eloquent full lips, and a perfectly aligned nose. She rarely wore make up; she didn't need to. She had a tiny frame for a woman of five feet seven, she cut her long brown hair shoulder length and set it in curls around her oblong face. A fashionable dresser, she wore knee-high skirts, bobby socks, and pretty blouses with scarves.

Dad is seven years older than Mom. They both went to school at the Holy Angels Mission in Fort Chipewyan. Grandma Isabelle, Dad's mom, had spent her childhood in the mission too. She later met Grandpa Emile, and they married and raised a family. In Grandma Isabelle's day, a young woman wasn't allowed to leave the mission until she was married. That changed in Mom's time. She was sent there at five and remained until she was sixteen, and then Mom and Dad fell in love on their own accord and got married. Dad wasn't in the mission as long as Mom. In fact, they didn't meet until they had left the mission; they met at a poker game. Mom lost her treaty rights when she married Dad.

Mom's dad, Grandpa Jonas, lived on a trapline most of his life, which was common then. He was a trapper and hunter. Eventually he moved to Fort Chipewyan. He had no choice in the matter of his children being placed in the mission. It was law that treaty Indians be apprehended to attend residential school. He and Granny Annie had twelve children; four survived tuberculosis.

Grandpa Jonas had concerns about Dad not being a trapper or hunter when Mom married him, but Dad worked hard to earn a living as a fisherman on the barge until he injured his arm. Then in 1952, his dad, Grandpa Emile, moved his family to Uranium City for work. Grandpa Emile was a professional cook, and was also known as a keen card player, gambler, pool shark and fiddler. He was also a fisherman and was skilled at the art of making traditional skiffs, a boat built by hand. There wasn't much he couldn't do.

Mom and Dad followed Grandpa Emile to Uranium City in the mid 1950s, but they didn't stay. They returned to Fort Chipewyan, and then in 1960 they moved back to Uranium City when Mom was pregnant with my oldest sister. Dad found work in the mine. He was the first Native man to work a hoister, breaking ground for other Native men to follow.

Dad was independent and industrious, and quick to learn every aspect of mining. He was a diamond driller too and earned himself a good reputation. After a serious mining accident, he became a heavy-duty mechanic and truck driver. Dad was a hard-working man who never let anything keep him down. No matter what happened, he worked.

Honeymoon-love carried them through their first years of marriage, and Dad earned good money and provided for his family while Mom stayed at home. They bought a beautiful house on a hill, complete with modern amenities, and by the time Mom was twenty-five she was busy with five little girls.

Then alcohol found its way into their nest, weakening its foundation. Their lives became immersed in heartache and chaos. Dad drank, and Mom found herself in a situation of "if you can't beat 'em, join 'em." Eventually she started drinking too. She hadn't been a drinker in her youth; in fact, she once aspired to become a nurse. Misery loves company, though, and with the pressure of being coaxed to have a drink once too often and needing to fit in, Mom picked up a beer one night and never put it down.

Maybe drinking numbed the pain when Dad became violent. Mom was on the receiving end of some vicious beatings. Inside the walls of their beautiful home, in between the parties, parenting, and work, Dad's wandering ways eventually got the best of him. He began to disappear for weeks and months at a time, usually leaving Mom with nothing more than tears to raise us girls on. Then out of the blue, he'd return like nothing had happened, and for a short time they resumed their lives – until the next time.

These turbulent times took their toll, and Mom soon began to shuffle us girls among relatives or friends when she went out during Dad's disappearances, sometimes looking for him, other times simply getting on with her life as a young single parent. When she realized she had to get used to fending for herself, she found a part-time job as a waitress in the hotel in Uranium City. We girls often sat at the counter eating french fries while waiting for her to finish her shift.

Mom finally left Dad after his family reported her to Social Services because Mom left us with Uncle Roger, Dad's younger brother. Social Services apprehended all five of us girls, placing us in different foster homes. Mom was outraged when she found out and went straight to Social Services, demanding to know where her girls were. They wouldn't tell her, so, without their permission, she found each of us and took us back. The oldest, Sara, was five, I was three, Carol was two, Bobbie was one, and Mom had just had the baby, Dora.

It was a good thing Mom came looking on account of the foster family that had Bobbie. They wanted to adopt her; in fact, Mom found Bobbie at the airport as the couple were attempting to leave Uranium City and return to Europe. Bobbie almost ended up living in another country. It was quite a scene when Mom took Bobbie back.

The foster family I lived with hid me in their basement when they heard Ann was looking for her girls. Even though they knew

Mom, they didn't want trouble from Social Services. When Mom found me there, she explained her circumstances to them; they empathized with her and didn't stop her from taking me back. Mom and Dad's problems were common knowledge in a town where everyone washed everyone else's dirty laundry.

Once she had rounded up her babies, Mom returned to Fort Chipewyan, where we moved in with Grandpa Jonas and Granny Annie in a bush tent in an area called Dog Head. The white canvas tent was home to Mom's younger brother Lance, Aunty Angeline, Grandpa Jonas, Granny Annie, and now Mom and her five girls. Mom didn't stay in Fort Chipewyan long, and I was separated from my sisters amidst the confusion of who could take care of which child when Mom decided to go back to Uranium City to settle matters.

In between Aunty Angeline and Granny Annie taking care of me, I ended up living with Granny Iyas. She was married to Grandpa Jacob, the brother of Jonas. She lived two hills over from Grandpa Jonas in a small shack on a hill. Dynamite comes in small packages, and Granny Iyas was five feet of spirit and fire. She dressed like most grannies in those days: She wore a skirt with a patterned polyester shirt, a sweater, beige stockings, and moccasins, and she pinned her hair back in a tight bun. I didn't know then that Granny Iyas was becoming more and more blind as a result of a cataract. She got around easily, not only taking care of herself and Grandpa Jacob, but me too. She spoke her mind and was mischievous. Granny Iyas was an animated teller of stories, which always made people laugh.

Her brother-in-law, my Grandpa Jonas, was a tall, lean man. His moccasins and rubbers, dark green cotton pants, plaid shirts, and cotton-brown tweed hat were his signature style. He walked like a bushman, aware of his surroundings and steady in his step. When he looked at me I felt cradled in his soul – connected. I was his daughter's child, and therefore we were his children too.

Living in the bush, in unison with nature and the elements, gave him a subtle strength. Grandpa Jonas was introspective, reserved in his power and personal truth; there was nothing foreign about him. He was natural. All the old folks were that way. Life's challenges were taken on without complaining or whining. Bear down and work, whether hunting or checking your traps – just do what needs to be done. My grannies tended to their beading, making moccasins, or mending clothes and blankets while the men did their chores.

The ability to laugh at oneself and make light of any situation kept everyone entertained in spite of hardships. Joking and teasing kept life in perspective. If you couldn't laugh at yourself, there was always someone willing to laugh at you or make fun of you until you lightened up. It was a skilled art of quick wit and keen observation of a person's weakness of character, and the joking either toughened you up or turned you into a whiner.

The old folks spoke Chipewyan. It was soothing to listen to their monotone voices of guttural melody and nasal sounds describing life surrounding us, bonding our link through our language. They listened to me tell stories too. I made them laugh. I didn't speak Chipewyan fluently, yet I understood when I was told to go to bed, when to eat, and if they were making fun of me. Speaking to me in Chipewyan validated me. I was of them, we were of the land, and together we belonged.

In between running back and forth between Granny Iyas's shack and Granny Annie's bush tent, life was simple. The wood-burning stove woke me at sunrise as the chirping of birds greeted a new dawn. Sometimes Aunty Angeline read comics to me, or I helped pick lint off sweaters and blankets. We girls kept busy chasing each other. Our days were spent in the hills or catching frogs from a pond, getting muddy, climbing trees, and skinning our knees. In the summer's womb of scents, fir, pine and spruce fragranced the hills, and wildflowers blossomed as bees suckled sweet nectar. At the mission playground we played on swings and ran from the big kids. A day usually ended with bumps and bruises.

I didn't take much notice of Mom being away when she left. My extended family replaced my natural yearning for Mom, and being a child, I lived in the moment. Laughter was louder than the loneliness for Mom and Dad.

When we got hungry, there was always bannock and baloney to eat. Bannock was cooked in a frying pan over a fire outside, along with meals of wild meat and fish throughout the day. With so many kids around, wieners and canned goods from the Bay were a convenience they couldn't afford yet managed to provide. Sometimes I was allowed to go to the Bay store with Grandpa Jonas; he bought chips and pop for me, and my grannies always had candy stashed somewhere.

As the leaves changed colour, it got colder at night, and by morning Granny Iyas's linoleum floor felt like I was walking on ice. Granny Iyas rose before the sun and made sure a fire was burning in the woodstove when I awoke. Then we would sit down for porridge, toast and tea as she quietly began her day in the kitchen. Morning was quiet time, so I knew to stay out of the way.

Granny Iyas wasn't used to a three-year-old craving her attention like a lost cub suckling for milk. Wiping my runny nose, washing my clothes, feeding me, finding me, having me tag along like a shadow, she spoke to me like an adult yet handled me like a child, setting right from wrong with a switch or sharp tongue when needed. I made her work hard when I wet the bed, and she washed my sheets regularly, which meant hauling water. Sometimes I was scared of her, yet I felt safe.

Early in the morning, Granny would send me to Grandpa Jonas's to play with my sisters; by noon, she'd come for me. For a little girl and her granny, our routine was simple. I played so she could make my bed and tend to her business or visit during the day.

Then, just as I was becoming accustomed to a serene life with Granny Iyas and Grandpa Jacob, Mom returned, and with her a whirlwind that would send me far away from the security I had settled into.

Bobbie and I were moving to Rae-Edzo in the Northwest Territories to live with Aunt May and Uncle Fred. Grandpa Jonas and Granny Annie would keep baby Dora, and my sisters Carol and Sara would go with Mom. She was moving back to Uranium City. I was happy Dora was staying with Grandpa and Granny. They wouldn't be so lonely.

At the airport Mom cried. I told her: "Don't cry Mommy, I'll send you some dry meat." She laughed as she wiped her tears and kissed us good-bye.

Living far away with Aunt May and Uncle Fred was loneliest at night. I thought of my grannies all the time. The wind whistled outside my bedroom window as the dogs howled, reminding me of home. I held close the memory of Granny Iyas's voice.

During the winter I got sick with pneumonia. That night an emergency flight had to be made from Yellowknife to Rae-Edzo, and back to a hospital in Yellowknife. It was forty below outside as I burned with fever, wrapped in blankets while they carried me onto the plane.

I awoke in the hospital. Aunt May was standing by my bed. I fell in and out of sleep as my fever dropped. I slept until the pneumonia was gone. Aunt May stayed with me as much as she could and whenever I woke to find her gone, I became scared. As soon as I felt better and before the nurses could turn their heads, I was running up and down the hallways, talking to people and asking the nurses a million questions:

"What happened to that person?"

"When can I go home?"

"Who is going to take me back to my Mommy?"

"How come I have to stay here?"

When I wasn't interrogating the nurses, I wandered the hallways. One day I saw a man who looked familiar, so I walked up to him from behind while he talked to another man, and I tugged on his leg.

"Are you my daddy?" I asked.

He looked down and grabbed me in his arms.

"Jolene?" he cried as he hugged me.

Dad had been in a serious mining accident. He'd been showing pictures of his girls to a buddy when I saw him. I was allowed to stay with him all day until I fell asleep. I argued to stay all night, but the nurse said, "Your Dad might roll over and squish you."

Dad said I talked like nobody's business. When the candy cart came by, he bought me anything I wanted, until the nurse asked him not to buy me too much candy. He did anyway.

For three days I snuggled close to Dad. I left kicking and screaming with my Aunt May after Dad tried to explain why I couldn't stay with him.

I don't remember much after leaving the hospital.

I was five when Aunt May and Uncle Fred brought us to Edmonton to be with Mom.

When Bobbie and I returned to Mom, she had had another baby. Ruth was number six. Mom lived in a high-rise apartment near the High Level Bridge, and once again all my sisters, except Dora, were together. My sister Carol started sleepwalking while we lived in this apartment. Sometimes she walked right out of the building and onto the streets and would wake up crying, but she always found her way home.

Mom had a regular babysitter, Shirley. She was at our apartment most of the time, sometimes for days. Shirley threw lots of parties. We hardly had food, and when Shirley ordered out for her and her friends, we were usually sent to bed without anything to eat.

Dad showed up one day, and this time he stayed for a while. He bought everything Mom needed – furniture, food – and gave her money to buy us clothes. They were out one night when Dad came home without Mom. He was sober. Shirley had sent us to bed long before he came home, and when he walked in, he found her balancing on the balcony rail, holding herself up with her fingertips on the balcony above.

I sneaked out of bed and peeked around the corner just as she was telling Dad, "I can fly!" He slowly moved toward her, grabbed her around the waist, then pulled her onto the balcony floor. She could hardly walk or stand when Dad sent her home in a taxi. When Mom got home, he became enraged at her for letting teenagers on drugs take care of us. When they started yelling and arguing, I went to bed.

Dad left after that. That's when we moved to a basement suite of an old house. Bikers and hippies lived above us. Sometimes they drank with Mom, but they mostly kept to themselves. Mom now had all of us back, including Dora. Dora didn't speak English very well because Grandpa Jonas and Granny Annic only spoke to her in Chipewyan, but she caught on fast.

It was from this house that I walked to the Cecil Hotel to find Mom.

We six girls were left alone more often than not, without a babysitter. One night, Aunt Angeline arrived unexpectedly to find all of us alone. When she tracked Mom down, Aunt Angeline threatened to report her to Social Services and told her she was taking the baby, Ruth, if Mom didn't come home.

Mom came home that night, but Aunt Angeline took Ruth the next day anyway. She lived in Prince Rupert, B.C., with her husband. Shortly after Aunt Angeline took Ruth, Bobbie and I were sent to live with Aunt May and Uncle Fred again. They now lived in St. Paul, Alberta. I liked living with them, but they couldn't replace the comfort of being with all my sisters. I missed their giggles and the reassurance we gave each other. Their faces mirrored me: teasing, crying, laughing big-belly-piss-your-pants laughter. Only sisters can do this, and each sister was like a spool of thread that stitched fragments of our ragged family quilt together.

I turned six in October and started school while living with Aunt May. I was anxious to get on with the business of learning how to read and write. I discovered that this wouldn't be the case in grade one, so one day I informed my teacher, "I didn't come to school to paint, draw and colour. I came to school to learn how to read and write." I kept complaining until the teacher placed me in grade two six weeks later.

Aunt May wasn't anything like Mom. She was shorter and plump. There was a resemblance in their eyes, but Aunt May wasn't as striking as Mom. She was stern and wore casual clothes that didn't flatter her. She was also soft spoken until angered; then everyone heard her.

My stubborn streak challenged Aunt May, especially when it came to going to church, where I squirmed and complained to no end. Then one Sunday I saw a cute boy and decided church wasn't so bad. His name was Paul.

My sister and I were sent to bed early every night after we cleaned up after ourselves. I argued to stay up to watch television until the strap came out. Aunt May only had to show it to me and I went to bed. Living with Mom, there wasn't a bedtime, mostly because we were left alone most of the time.

In bed, I'd wait for everyone to fall asleep so I could tiptoe downstairs and kiss Paul's picture. His family were friends of Aunt May and Uncle Fred. Much to my delight, they had given us their family photo for Christmas.

I could tell Aunt May was upset when she hung up the phone one afternoon. I overheard her tell Uncle Fred that Mom wanted us back. The thought of being with all my sisters made me happy.

Once again Aunt May packed us up and drove us to Edmonton to live with Mom.

Two years after my baby sister Ruth was taken away, Mom was pregnant with number seven. Mom was twenty-eight. We were together again, except for Ruth. We lived in an area of Edmonton called Little Italy. Dad began making appearances again, but he never stayed longer then a few days. When he did come, he bought groceries and most everything we needed at the time. We kept him busy as we competed for his attention.

Then, one night in June, Mom left, and Dad took care of us. Days later, Mom pulled up in a taxi carrying a baby. We rushed to the door to meet our new sister, Tania. Dad stayed and Mom left – she had to leave us with dad because he was threatening to throw Tania away. When Mom came back from Vancouver, Dad left. It was a good thing he did because they'd fought all the time and he'd hit Mom. I was scared of Dad when he became angry; I was thrown across the room once when we lived in the apartment.

We girls argued among ourselves over who would carry Tania. When we weren't fighting, we'd play in the park, where we befriended two Italian boys; their dad owned a grocery across the street from the park. A girl named Karen lived at the end of our block. She was always at our house. Her mom drank lots too and hit her, so she spent most of her time with us. Karen was skinny with light brown hair. Her clothes were always dirty, like her, and she looked sad most of the time. I liked her, but sometimes we picked on her for no reason. She still came around; she had nowhere else to go. Karen was the same age as my sister Dora.

My sisters and I were like steps in age and height. The oldest, Sara, was bigger than everyone, and a bully. When Mom wasn't home, she'd make everyone clean while she'd lie around, and she didn't waste time in beating us up if we didn't listen. But she was the smartest in school.

Then there was me. Dad used to tease me, telling me I had small eyes and big ears, like a mouse. I got mad one day and, before storming out, told him, "I look funny because I look like you!" I didn't like being called 'monkey ears' by my sisters, and once I locked them in the bathroom for hours because they were teasing me. I had a broom, and when they tried to open the door, I poked them. They stopped calling me 'monkey ears'.

Carol was pretty and skinny. Mom said she looked like one of her late sisters. Carol had light brown hair and fair skin. She could run fast, and when she got mad, she held her own in a fight. Carol and Sara were close.

Bobbie was tall and skinny too. We looked alike, but she was prettier and didn't have big ears or small eyes.

Dora looked like Aunt May.

Ruth was the most beautiful, and Tania was the cutest. Aunty Angeline let Ruth visit us, and when Ruth came home with her nice clothes we'd pick on her until she cried. When we were all home, Mom started taking more nerve pills.

Our Italian neighbours were loud too, and fought like Mom and Dad when he was home. If there was a contest on whose family was the loudest on the block, the neighbours would have won. Their mom didn't talk, she screamed. I could hear her from inside our house. I learned how to swear in Italian. They had a lot of kids too, and sometimes we played; most of the time we fought.

Mom didn't work. She got welfare to help her, and at Christmas, Santas Anonymous dropped off bags filled with presents, and a turkey dinner came in a food hamper. We girls shared a hand-me-down wardrobe, raided gardens, and collected pop bottles. When left alone to fend for ourselves, we tore the house apart. As Mom's drinking worsened along with her consumption of nerve pills, we became ruthless in our efforts to keep her home, misbehaving while desperately seeking her attention, which only drove Mom crazier.

I was in grade three when we moved from Little Italy to a house in the northeast end of the city, near 118 Avenue and 72 Street. It had three bedrooms and a spacious basement. The kitchen was beside the living room. The emptiness of the house felt like the lonely streets of the city at night. It was like the television – the loud noise kept my attention but it only made me feel lonelier. We didn't have much for furniture, other than what we needed: a used couch and chair that didn't match, a coffee table, a kitchen table and chairs. The beds were used too; most everything we owned was bought from a second-hand store or given to us.

In this neighbourhood there were kids all around us. The neighbours living in a house across the alley from us knew Mom from Uranium City; they had three kids. Our next-door neighbours on our right had two girls our age, Jackie and Jill.

I liked the newness of everything; it was exciting. I wanted to discover everything around me, to find out who lived in our neighbourhood and meet them, which I did. Halfway down the block lived an elderly couple, Mr. and Mrs. Books. They gave us their empties once they had become accustomed to our tapping on their door asking for bottles. They overlooked our raids on their apple tree most of the time. Mr. Books always seemed to know when we girls were left alone, which was most of the time, and that's when he'd show up at our door with a bag of groceries.

Our house was a jungle of activity when we were left alone, six girls wildly rampaging. The television was our babysitter. Food commercials made me hungry. When everyone fell asleep, I remained awake, waiting, always waiting for Mom to come home. Every car that drove by kept me alert and hopeful that it was Mom in a taxi. She never owned a car.

Although I was only second oldest, I took on the responsibility of making sure everyone was taken care of. That is, when Sara and I weren't trying to kill each other. One time she left me locked out until I smashed the front door window with my fist, causing a deep cut in the palm of my hand. My retaliation was a pair of scissors aimed at her head. I missed and had to sleep in the garbage bin that night, hiding from her.

In our effort to occupy ourselves, we explored the area we lived in. A few blocks away there was a meat factory near a railway, which became territory for a fortress where witches and goblins lived. I created a magical world there with my mystical powers. Those were lazy, playful days.

I got around the city on the bus. Number 5 brought me all the way downtown to where Uncle Fred and Aunt May now lived. I spent as much time with them as possible, or Mom would send me there for groceries or money.

It was while we lived in this house that we met our stepdad, Jake. He'd been one of the many people Mom brought home with a party, and then one day, he was passed out in bed with Mom. After a few weeks, I knew he wasn't going anywhere.

I felt uneasy around him. He looked to me like a pitbull, walking pigeon-toed with clenched fists. His stocky upper body appeared hard as steel. He wore tight jeans with biker boots and cheesy cowboy shirts that were unbuttoned too low.

Having Jake around meant that Dad came back less often.

Mom had brought home relatives before, or people she'd met at the bar and partied with. Anything she had to offer, she gave. She was kind-hearted. Our house was a soup-and-bannock hostel to anyone she deemed in need, and there were lots of strangers and relatives in need of a place to stay, or people looking for a party.

THE PIPER

I was eight. I'd lie in bed listening to familiar drunken slurs of loud voices competing to be heard. Beer caps popped off bottles. Whiskey bottles slammed on the table as strangers guzzled booze while country-and-western music bounced bass tones off the living room window. Despite the noise, my heavy eyelids soon closed; the voices disappeared.

I had a nightmare.

I was cold when I opened my eyes. A man was touching my privates. My bottom pyjamas were off while he moaned and kept rubbing me and himself. Awake, I screamed until Mom ran to the bedroom. I choked in between sobs, trying to tell Mom what the man had done to me. He shook his head in denial of my accusations as I lay in bed with my bottom pyjamas and panties off.

I knew she believed me. There was brimstone in her eyes.

She grabbed a whiskey bottle and smashed it over his head as he ran out of the bedroom. In her rage, she yelled at me to get to bed and chased after him.

I'm looking at you looking at me and I want to know why I'm not myself in your eyes anymore. Was it something I did? Is it my fault? Am I as dirty as the look you give me now? Mommy, I couldn't stop

*him. I was sleeping when he came. His thing was in his hand when I
woke up screaming. It must have been a bad dream. I'm looking at
you looking at me and I want to know why I'm not myself in your eyes
anymore.*

It was never mentioned again.

The denial of this event was a crazy-making menace in my
mind, so I retreated within myself and discovered the celestial
heavens in the neighbours' back yard. I used their swing set in the
middle of the night. Rocking back and forth, watching the stars,
waiting for Mom to come home as loneliness and hunger kept me
awake, I sang, "Twinkle-twinkle, little star... Up above the world
so high..." reciting the song over and over to myself.

When I couldn't stay awake on the swing, I made my way back
to the house, to my bedroom. I opened the curtains so I could see
the stars from my bedroom window. I felt connected to the stars;
they were there for me no matter what, and with them I drifted far
away to a safe place. With the stars watching over me in my bedroom, I knelt like I remembered Aunt May did in church, and
prayed. Squeezing my eyes tightly, my prayers were simple. "God,
please bring Mommy home. If she won't come home, keep her
safe." I asked God to take care of my sisters, "Tell Mommy to bring
milk for the baby, " and "Send someone to take care of us."

There were even prayers to take her away forever so we could
live with a nice family.

I didn't get angry with God for seemingly not listening. I just
figured I wasn't that important.

In my magical midnight world, I talked to the stars, spirits,
imaginary people and angels. I'd talk and talk, gibberish, much
about nothing, mostly to keep my mind quiet as I sewed doll
clothes. I was always making something or taking something
apart. Rags came from anyone's clothes, if the pattern was one
I liked. When I got bored with ripping apart clothes and sewing,
I'd pretend to be a playschool teacher; my sisters were my

students. Forts were built with sheets in the basement, living room or anywhere deemed suitable for a fort, which was decorated with everything I could fit inside. If something was lost, it was likely in the fort, my secret hiding place.

I preferred being alone, safely hidden in a world of make believe where no one could penetrate my secret haven. In my mind, I lived in isolation, where I regressed further into myself in my darkest waking moments.

The first time Jake came to my bed, I pretended to be asleep as his beer breath moved close to my face. He roughly groped my body with his calloused hands. I choked in terror and disbelief, then opened my eyes. He covered my mouth until I could barely breathe, and made me promise to be quiet or he'd hurt me. Only then did he allow me to breathe again.

Frozen in terror, I wondered where Mommy was.

After that, I lay quiet while Jake sexually abused me. He'd push his fingers hard in my privates as I squirmed and fought back, as he covered my mouth until his smell and insane eyes paralysed me. The more I fought, the more he liked it. I stopped fighting back, which made him angrier. I knew he was finished when he groaned and then zipped up his pants. He'd put his finger to his lips, gesturing for me to remain quiet. I wanted to die as my insides curdled from Jake's touch.

The next day, in order to face Jake and Mom, I'd act like nothing had happened. But my body told the truth, and when I saw Jake I became nauseous. It took everything I had to forget what he'd done in the middle of the night as my sisters and Mom slept. No matter how hard I tried, I couldn't erase the memory. At school, I sat in class raw and bruised from the inside out, as I faded farther and farther into myself, until I couldn't hear anyone talk to me.

Brown-eyed girl you're so far away today. Can you play?
I can't play today. I have a secret.
I know where the Piper goes in the middle of the night. He pulls
me inside out as he whistles in my ear. You can't follow me there. It's
not safe to play with the Piper.
I have a secret. I'm hiding from the Piper today, so go away.

In class I watched children. Their voices became slow, shallow sounds as I shrank smaller and smaller. I was a tiny ant crawling on the seat of my chair, small and insignificant as the clock ticked, dull and hypnotic, like the teacher, and then the school bell jolted me back to size. School was out.

Jake continued coming back to my bed. During the day, he'd watch me and smile when I looked at him, making my tummy hurt until I held my breath for the feeling to stop.

From a distance, standing in the same room with him, I'd listen to his laughter that made Mom laugh too. I saw my sisters play together as I stood watching everyone happily carry on with the day while I melted into the skin I couldn't escape from. The scene appeared like nothing was wrong, and if there was, it was because I was too emotional, too sensitive, always crying for nothing.

I kept my promise and didn't say anything to anyone. My desire to learn faded. I could pretend nothing was wrong until it seemed nothing *was* wrong.

When Mom and Jake were sober, they got along. It was like he was two different people. I'd watch him around my sisters; he didn't look at them like he looked at me. Maybe I did something wrong to make him hurt me. I must be bad.

Tick-tock-tick-tock – time to wake and wait. Does he remember
like I do what he does? Can he see through me? Does he know I know?
Crunch-crunch-cereal, here he comes. He's hung over. Let's pretend
again – It didn't happen again – I hate him – Is it bad to wish he
were dead? – He won't look at me – I know he knows I know – Hate

is all I feel and it's too late, too late for school – My tummy is tight –
I'm a bad girl – Bad girls are dirty – Don't look at me or I'll puke...

Walking to school a ticking time bomb of rage, I could taste the hate boiling in me as I marched on, wanting to hit something or someone. I felt ugly and dirty. Then at school I'd worry about Mom, if she was home watching Tania. Not knowing made me angrier and anxious to get home, so I would act sick when I couldn't sneak out of class.

In class I started coughing. Faking a cold, I coughed and coughed until I was sent to see the nurse. In her office I coughed more, trying to look like I was in pain. The nurse watched me. I caught her glance and then rolled over in agony, coughing and pleading to go home. The nurse looked me square in the eye and said, "You're a good actor... So good, in fact, you can go home."

What I found once I got home varied. Sometimes it was a good thing I had left school, because Tania or my other sisters were left alone; other times all I found was a mess to clean up while everyone remained passed out.

I had other reasons for wanting to stay away from school. There was a bully in fifth grade who would beat me up after school. He easily outran me, so I found different routes home. Still, he usually found me and left me in tears after a good licking. With kids at school calling me names, the more Mom and Jake fought, I began to hit before I got hit. I started beating up kids in between being bullied myself. I had my own victims: a little Italian girl in particular. I envied her for her perfect dresses and shoes. All the kids liked her, but when I found her alone, she wasn't left looking so pretty.

In class, the teacher talked about history and Indians. She referred to Indians as "people who needed to be civilized." That's why there were so many wars. Indians were killing innocent people who settled here. All I could think about was Grandpa Jonas and all the Indians in my family. When I told the teacher

Indians didn't kill people like she said, she scolded me in front of the class. Afterward, my classmates teased me and said, "You're stupid because you're an Indian."

And all the nice things teachers told me about how smart I was didn't matter anymore. I didn't fit in, except in drama and art where we played and made things up. I was good at that. For a little while I could impress the teacher and other kids with my acting and artwork. Being poor and not having new clothes or nice shoes didn't bother me when I joined in fun games with other kids. They noticed me and I could hide how I felt inside.

The teacher made an announcement in art class. There was going to be a poster contest for the fire hall in our neighbourhood. We had to draw pictures about what to do if there was a fire. Two weeks later the winners were announced in class. When the teacher called the first-place winner to the front of the class I sat in my chair. The teacher called again. I remained in my seat until I finally heard her calling my name. I had won first place! I got up and walked to the front of the class, shy at first, in disbelief, and the teacher proudly described why I had won first place. She displayed my poster in front of everyone, noting how careful I had been to describe several fire exits in an apartment building and how to use them safely to escape a fire, explaining to the class how clever it was of me to talk about what not to do as well. She said that the picture of a fireman carrying a little girl and her dog from a burning building and her family happy to see that she was safe was very well drawn. As the teacher bragged about my artwork, I stood taller, until I beamed a great big toothy smile. After class, some kids said I was a good artist and that it was the best poster.

I ran all the way home to show Mom and Jake my poster, excited because there was going to be a fancy ceremony and the winners could invite their family and friends. The firemen would give the first-, second- and third-place winners their prize at the ceremony. At home I told Mom all about it and begged her to be there. She said she would. I couldn't wait.

On the morning of the ceremony, Mom was hung over as she dressed me in my nicest dress, curling my hair and fastening it with barrettes that matched my blue dress. Mom even bought me a pair of shiny new black shoes with silver buckles, which I wore with new white leotards. When I left for school, Mom promised me she would be there. All day in class I waited until it was time to go to the church where the ceremony would be held.

When we got there, I sat alone in the back. All the other winners' families and friends started arriving as I waited for Mom to walk in. The church was full of students and some teachers, the principal, firemen, and my art teacher. Mom didn't show up, and when the principal called my name, I shyly accepted my award from a fireman while trying not to cry. I walked to my seat, ignoring the applause and people who watched me walk to the empty row where I sat while the others kids were surrounded by their families.

When I got home, Mom and Jake were drinking, and no one asked me about the ceremony. I got mad, and before I went to bed I yelled at Mom for forgetting.

When the teacher congratulated me again the next day, I ignored her. She pinned my poster up in the classroom, but when I looked at it, the special feeling I once had was gone. I told myself it was a stupid contest anyway.

At home, our house remained a circus full of drunkards, with little if any food and dirty sheets. Peeing in bed wasn't unusual; the smell of beer was stronger than the mess left behind.

There came a time when I looked forward to Mom and Jake leaving. Sometimes they'd be gone for days, but when they were gone too long, I got scared again.

I stood at my post by the window in the middle of the night, lonely and, at times, afraid they would return.

If Mom and Jake were home, violence ensued, and I crawled deeper into my fantasy world. Mom's screams reverberated like church bells in my head every time Jake punched her out, and like a wild cougar she defended herself until he beat her into submission. And each time I witnessed the horror of this violence against my mother, the wires in my head short-circuited, scrambling my brain as I watched and waited for the chaos to end. Most days she was recognizable, but she usually had bruises or a battered face.

Mom moved more often now that Jake lived with us. Sometimes they were evicted because of parties or violence. Other times they wanted to start over, which meant new schools and more confusion. My grades were poor, and I didn't want to be around other kids because I felt different. I just wanted to be left alone.

I kept my secret, never telling anyone, especially my sisters. I was afraid they would tell on me, and then what would Jake do? As often as I could get away from him and home, I did.

Sara and I fought all the time. She was bigger and stronger, taxing my fast and vicious responses, so I started running away. I'd leave home not knowing where I'd end up. At the mall, I'd watch people, wishing for parents to take me shopping too. Hunger pangs shrank my stomach. My hair was stringy and greasy. I might have bathed a few days ago. I felt ugly and invisible.

The fights between Sara and me got worse when Mom stayed away, until all I did was run away and skip school because I had nothing to eat and nothing clean to wear. I knew no one would be worried or care about where I was, so I did whatever I wanted to do, which usually ended with me in trouble.

The only other kid on the block who got more attention than me for being bad was a plump Italian boy we nicknamed Pizza.

He lived at the end of our block. Pizza caused a few riots. One time he collected a jar of worms, caterpillars and bugs, and when Mom and her girlfriend were sunbathing, he sneaked up on them and threw the jar of insects all over Mom's friend while she was napping. The whole block heard her screaming. Pizza didn't come around for a few weeks afterward.

Across the street from us, Macy, who was my age, lived with her mom. I liked Macy's mom because she always invited me for supper, and now and then Macy came over for bannock. One day Macy's mom asked for the recipe for bannock. I told her I would ask my mom but I kept forgetting. After being asked for the recipe once too often, I told Macy's mom, "Our great Indian chief said we're not allowed to give the recipe away." Macy's mom stared at me blankly and then laughed aloud. It wasn't brought up again.

Kitty-corner from our block was a white picket fence with a white-and-blue house in a well-kept yard where a young couple lived with their daughter, Tammy. In my estimation, Tammy had everything a girl could dream of, including a Barbie house complete with Ken and Barbie clothes. I'd go over to play with Tammy and pretend I lived there and we'd bake cakes in her Easy-Bake Oven. Sometimes a boy I liked would play with us at her house too.

One day I went over to Tammy's and when she came to the door I asked if I could play with her. She said no because her mom wasn't home and then closed the door. I peeked in her basement window and she was playing with the boy I liked. I banged on the door and when she answered, I asked her to come outside. I had something to give her. She did.

I proceeded to beat her up. The boy came out and stood by helplessly as he watched me give her one last punch. Shaking, the boy stammered, "You... you Indians sure are strong."

Trembling as I walked up to him, I kissed him on the lips and ran home as fast as I could. He was crying when Tammy's mom pulled into their driveway. When I eventually showed up at their house again, I wasn't allowed to play with Tammy any more and was told to go home. I never saw the little boy again.

Throughout my mishaps, adventures and well-intentioned plots of heroism, we also had to contend with the babysitters, friends Mom had grown up with in the Holy Angels Mission. I always eavesdropped when they visited, and the story was usually the same. There was always a man who had wronged them, or whom they had done wrong by, depending on who told the story. They also gathered at the Cecil Hotel, drinking draft beer while talking beer-talk about the old days.

Among these women, we children were rounded up and left to fend for ourselves at one of their houses. The eldest child, usually no more than eleven or twelve and as young as nine, was left responsible for the remaining crew of children. There could be four to eight children left alone on weekends. The television was our babysitter.

Mom's friends took turns hosting the kids, which meant more travelling around the city with my sisters in tow. Over time I lost track of where we were supposed to be and with whom.

The only difference it made was when it was Agnes's house. I didn't like her, and it was mutual. It never took Agnes long to head out the door, and when she left, it usually meant being alone with all the kids for more then a night. Once, I decided to leave after she had been out all night. I brought my sisters home with me. When we got home, the house was locked, so we broke in, and then I searched the empty cupboards for something to eat. I saw that we had flour, lard, baking powder, and salt. This was all we needed to make bannock, so I phoned Aunt May and lied to her: "Mom forgot how to make bannock and she needs the recipe." Aunt May played along. She instructed me over the phone on what to do and within an hour showed up at our house with groceries.

Aunt May got there in time. The bannock was burning. It was hard as a rock and tasted like glue. I had made a mess in the kitchen, which she made me clean up, and then she stayed with us until Mom and Jake came home. They had a good laugh, overlooking the fact we had run away from Agnes and broken into our own house. Agnes didn't find it so funny.

When it came to eating, I found ways. The milkman's empty milk bottles had money in them if I got to the bottles early enough on schooldays. At school, I'd tell the teacher I needed to go to the bathroom and then eat other kid's lunches in the coatroom.

The easiest way to find money was breaking into neighbourhood homes when people were at work or on holidays. If I had enough money, I bought bread and baloney for my sisters, who wouldn't try any of my approaches to finding money or food. Shoplifting wasn't as easy as break and enters, but stealing from stores didn't make me feel as bad.

As Jake's violence and sexual abuse increased at home, I took it out on other kids, at home and at school. He wasn't the only predator. There were others. It depended on who was at the party or who was babysitting us. A teenaged girl who babysat us made me touch her body. I didn't want to do all the things she wanted me to do, so I stopped. It was the only time someone listened when I asked them to stop touching me. Otherwise, my imagination took me far away from sexual abuse as I held my breath and waited for it to finish.

Eventually I couldn't cry anymore.

My tears stopped.

Hiding in a coffin, my body is a corpse to entertain demons clawing my skin. Silence numbs the pain. My spirit is no longer with me. Where I go, no one knows, floating over my body as another takes me in his grip, raping and ripping rotten flesh to fulfil his hunger for a child. I will cry no more for the body I once knew to be mine. Take me if you want; I'm the walking dead, here no more. I am numb and silent and you can't hurt me. I cannot afford to feel fear.

With another move to another different neighbourhood in Edmonton, I had to start at a new school. On the first day, I walked in late. All the kids stared at me, and then a freckled-faced boy said aloud, "Hey Squaw, can't you tell time?" The laughter grew louder. Something shattered in me as I stood in the front of the class ashamed, until a slow, burning rage surfaced. The teacher was gone, so I walked up to the boy, punched him in the head, and through clenched teeth said, "I'll see you after school." A silent shock swept over the room as I sat in an empty desk and waited for the teacher to arrive, anticipating a visit to the office.

No one said anything when the teacher came in.

The boy didn't show up after school and he never spoke to me again. In fact, few kids spoke to me that year, unless I spoke to them first. The schoolyard was my turf, and how I reigned depended on how I was treated at home. Still, I did whatever I could to avoid school. I couldn't concentrate on schoolwork if my life depended on it. When the teacher asked why I was late for school or why I hadn't completed my homework, I entertained my teacher and classmates with fantastic tales of life at home. I couldn't do my homework because my dad had joined the circus and I had to help feed the animals. A monkey got free and we had to chase it around the city. We found the monkey before Dad had to leave, and when he comes back, he's taking me to Disneyland.

My stories made everyone laugh, and I enjoyed the attention. The kids in class would later tell me what a great storyteller I was and laugh when they saw me.

Every time Jake sexually abused me, I was left in a daze of confusion. I didn't like feeling out of control at school; it made me feel crazy and stupid. I especially didn't like that other kids were laughing at me when I couldn't remember what I had said, until I didn't want to go to school at all because I was afraid of what I would say in class. Yet, no matter what I did, Mom made sure I went. Playing hooky was pointless; she always found out, so I made things up. I threw myself in a puddle of mud, ripped my pants, skinned my knee, and went home crying hysterically. I told Mom I had been hit by a car. It almost backfired. She wanted a description of the vehicle, so I described an old man driving a blue car and begged her not to phone the police. I just needed to stay home for the day.

My sisters and I ruled the neighbourhood. I was known for being tough, with attitude, swearing and fighting all the time without regard, and one day while walking home from babysitting Aunt Mary's kids and my sisters, a girl who lived across the street from us starting calling us dirty Indians and wagon burners. I was used to this kind of racial slur, but that day, I wasn't in the mood. I threatened to beat her up if I ever saw her again. She got scared and called her mom. It ended with the girl's mother at our door, calling my mom out. They resolved the squabble over beer.

My violent rampages increased as things worsened at home, until most kids wouldn't play with me. I was too unpredictable.

HOUSE OF HORRORS

Mom and Jake were gone for longer periods of time, which meant occasional walks down the drag to search for her in bars. I usually had the kids with me. We'd start at the York Hotel and make our way to the International Hotel, hitting most of the bars along 97 Street. Some days, the walk brought us to the Cecil Hotel. Sometimes we lucked out and found her. Other times, finding her wasn't a case of being lucky at all because we couldn't convince her to come home.

The concrete path toward finding Mom was worn. Empty, unfamiliar faces of strangers, drunk or sober, didn't faze me. I wasn't afraid. Only once did a pervert attempt anything, and it wasn't even on the drag. I was walking home from babysitting when a man asked if he could take my panties off and have sex with me. I replied by flinging a Pepsi bottle at his head and running home when the bottle hit him.

One day we five scruffy street kids waited in the York Hotel lobby for Mom's exit from the bar that swallowed her on welfare day. We asked the desk clerk to page her. As we sat in the lobby, an old drunkard staggered in off the street, swaying back and forth in an effort to reach the front desk. From the entrance through the lobby and to the desk was about five metres. Midway he paused. He leaned to the left, then slowly to the right, and, reaching into his pocket, he pulled out a thick wad of twenty-dollar bills. Bobbie zoned in on the sixty dollars that floated onto the carpet, about a metre from the desk and a little farther from my sister, whose eyes were as big as an owl's.

The drunkard reached the front desk as we held our collective breath. Before I could look down, Bobbie's big foot was on the money. It took her two seconds to manoeuvre the money from under her shoe into her pocket. He paid for his room and shuffled on. The desk clerk ignored us, but turned his back, smiling.

We exchanged anxious looks and ran out of the lobby, forgetting why we were there. We watched *Star Wars* twice that day, gorging on popcorn and pop, and had money left over to buy food.

Between the ages eight and nine, I lost track of how many times we moved from neighbourhood to neighbourhood. With every move, the only thing that changed was the address; the violence, poverty and sexual abuse continued, until it was all I knew. I'd wake up only to survive another day.

Home became a zoo, and we were caged with a predator. From the outside looking in, our lives didn't appear any different from our neighbours'. But from my perspective, life was dark and hopeless, and no one knew. No one could see what it was like.

The hope of being rescued from Jake arrived one night when I heard Mom and Jake arguing about Dad. Jake left that night. Dad arrived by morning, and this time he stayed for more than a night and Jake didn't come back.

Dad took us shopping for clothes at the Army and Navy store. Our fridge was filled with more food than I'd seen at one time, and Mom didn't drink so heavily while Dad was home.

We shared our own moments alone too. I curled up beside his big belly on the couch as we watched TV, and I fell sound asleep in his arms. I hadn't felt safe for so long that I had forgotten what calm felt like.

Dad had been home for a week when one night I woke up and bolted out of bed. I must have sensed something was wrong. I reached the stairwell just as Dad was walking out the door with his suitcase in hand.

I stood at the top of the stairs. He saw me. Time froze, but then he turned his back and continued walking out the door as though I wasn't there. I screamed, "Daddy, don't go!" and raced down the stairs in a panic, grabbed onto his neck, wrapped myself around him and held on with everything I had.

Mom pulled me off. I fought her, but she wouldn't let me go until he was out the door. When she let go, I ran after him, but he wouldn't stop walking away. I cried, "Daddy, don't leave! Take me with you...," until his large frame disappeared into a shadow and all I heard were his cowboy boots clicking on pavement a block away.

Mom came outside and pulled me up from the sidewalk. She let me sleep with her that night. The next day Jake came home. Mom kept me home from school, and I cried all day, sleeping between waking moments of realizing that Dad was gone again. I fell into a deep depression.

I waited for Dad to come back for months, but he didn't. The only thing worse than missing Dad was having Jake back. Missing school didn't matter to me anymore, and I couldn't have cared less if I ever went back when the school year ended.

We moved again.

This time we lived near skid row, two blocks from the York Hotel, at the bottom of society's economic ladder, drunken Indians on welfare. I didn't give a fuck. I was past the point of caring, and besides, in our neighbourhood, no one gave a rat's ass about anything, least of all image. This house felt as rotten as my innards. The spirit of the house spoke of lost transients coming and going, and the walls were worn and tattered, like the people who lived here. We were all merely existing.

There had been so many houses, and this wasn't one of the nicer ones. It was the poorest neighbourhood we'd lived in yet. I was just another kid from "the wrong side of the tracks," and I lost myself in our seedy neighbourhood amongst prostitutes, drunks and drug dealers.

There was nothing romantic about where we lived, and I knew it. We lived on the main floor of a house. The kitchen was in the back. We girls shared one bedroom, and Mom and Jake had their own room off the living room. The bathroom was small and built beneath the stairs going to the apartment above.

It was after midnight when they returned drunk one night, arguing as they walked in. We all ran to the door to see Mom and stopped dead in our tracks when we saw Jake. He had a crazed look in his eyes, so we scurried like mice to our hiding places, underneath beds, in closets, anywhere.

Within seconds he had Mom on the floor, kicking her. From beneath my bed, I could hear Mom fight back until the only sound I heard was her body being thrashed around. She stopped screaming. There was nothing but her groans of pain, which became gasps for breath, until I couldn't hear anything but the heaviness of his boots kicking her.

We all ran out of our hiding places and into the kitchen. The table was broken and the chairs turned over, charting the trail that Jake had made as he brutally beat Mom. Blood was everywhere. Mom's face was swollen beyond recognition as she lay unconscious in a pool of blood.

I thought she was dead.

Instinctively reacting in Mom's defence, Tania, who was three years old, charged at Jake, who was standing over Mom's body. She screamed as she hit him with her tiny enraged fists. He pushed Tania aside, and we all attacked him, but he hurled us around the kitchen like rag dolls.

Bobbie raced out the door to phone the police at the corner phone booth.

When Jake heard sirens from the police car pulling into our back alley, he ran out the door. Mom regained consciousness with a fright, jumped up, and grabbed a knife without thinking, screaming, "Where is he?" Startled, we started to cry from the insanity of everything.

She was still raring to fight when the police arrived. The expressions on the policemen's faces made me angrier. They were disgusted more than concerned. They tried to calm Mom down enough to take the knife away from her while another officer took notes. They offered to call an ambulance, but Mom shrugged them off and wouldn't cooperate.

Then, out of nowhere, Dad was standing at the door, shaking his head in dismay at the sight of blood everywhere. We stood in shock, crying after our mutiny against Jake's violence. He calmly informed the police who he was, and that he didn't live with us but he knew who was responsible for this. He reassured them everything would be okay now that he was there. Dad grabbed a towel, wet it, and gave it to Mom. She moaned as she held onto her ribs. He put Mom's arm over his shoulder and walked her to the bathroom to wash up.

Sara took the little girls to the bedroom as I picked up the chairs, ignoring the police as they talked on their radio. Dad came back and the police asked for a description of Jake. They told Dad that Social Services had been notified and would be arriving by noon to apprehend the kids. Dad offered to pack our things and wait until they arrived. He told the police that he understood and it was best if they left so he could get everyone ready. They hesitated until Dad strongly urged them to find Jake and arrest him.

When they were gone, Dad didn't waste any time. He rushed to the bedroom, grabbed a suitcase and yelled at us to grab anything we could find to wear and take with us while he packed Mom's clothes.

He drove all night until we arrived in Fort McMurray.

The next few weeks were a blur. Before I knew what had happened, Mom had moved us back to Edmonton with Jake. Dad was out of the picture, and with him, all hope.

Nothing changed.

Jake still lived in the house of horrors we had lived in before Dad rescued us that night, only now we lived on the second floor. It smelled of mildew, with a faint scent of urine lingering in the walls because the house had been unkempt. The kitchen sink was rusty and as ancient as the house, with plumbing that groaned and dripped, staining the sink. The tile floors were scuffed and looked dirty no matter how much they were washed.

This house had three levels. The first level was our old place. The second level had a living room, bathroom, kitchen, and two bedrooms. My bedroom was on the third level. The fire exit stairwell was in the back of the house; our bedroom had a door that led onto it, but it wasn't safe to walk on. I shared it with Bobbie and any sister who needed to feel safe. We often curled up together in one bed for comfort.

Shortly after we moved upstairs, a young couple rented the main floor of the house. The walls were so paper-thin we could hear Sharon and Larry talk downstairs. Sharon had one son, Mark, and sometimes I babysat him. He was two years old.

Sharon was beaten as often as Mom. Larry was a mean son of a bitch. He was skinny and lanky, with huge brown eyes that didn't appear to see anything but the explosion in his head when he was on heroin. Then he'd fall back in his chair, his mouth wide open, moving slowly and talking in a language of his own.

This was his usual state.

Or he would pace back and forth like a caged rat, irritated and scratching everywhere; then he usually beat Sharon for their welfare money. They were poor too, and Sharon took a lot of beatings so she could keep enough money to feed Mark. I walked in on him once. He had a rubber band tied on his arm and needle in his hand. Larry yelled at me, "Get the fuck out!" I swore back and left.

When he was sane, he complimented me on my figure, or my cute "button breasts." My body was starting to develop, as I grew awkwardly fast. I didn't like it because I could feel him peering at me, undressing me with his eyes as he suggested, "If you were a little older, I'd be pounding your door down." This sent chills down my spine every time.

The house reverberated with disturbing screams from Sharon or Mom, sirens and doors being pounded on in the middle of the night, children weeping and babies crying.

My sister Bobbie kicked a hole in the drywall in our bedroom, then placed her bed against it. It was our hiding place. When Jake got violent, we crawled into the crevice in the wall that led onto a small triangle perch on the roof. There was enough room for everyone. Sometimes Mom hid too.

Not being in my body was as easy as escaping or hiding. If I allowed myself to be in my body, I walked around like a zombie stuck in three states of existence: threatened, terrified or angry. When my sisters and I weren't in survival mode, we monitored the scale of potential attack. Yet regardless of my efforts to hide, Jake found me.

I was taking a bath one day when Jake walked in the bathroom. I pulled my knees close to my chest to cover my body. He stared at me and then picked up my panties from the floor and smelled them, wanting to know why they were so crusty.

The warm water turned into liquid nitrogen the moment I realized he was sober, leaving me unable to scream or speak as he stood over me. Seconds turned into hours as he raped me with a stare, rubbing his groin in his jeans, satisfied with himself as I sat naked in the tub.

Then I heard the thumping of feet walking up the stairs. I sat in the tub, rotting in my skin.

Jake smirked and said, "Maybe next time I'll get lucky. You should lock the door." He walked out of the bathroom smirking.

I felt dirtier, and no amount of soap could wash me clean as I scrubbed myself raw. My unclean panties lay on the floor, and I cried because they were all I had and I couldn't wear them after he'd touched them. I robotically stepped out of the tub, wrapped myself in a towel, and then sat on the floor fixated on the door. To myself, I whispered, "I thought no one was home, asshole."

Jake had told Mom he was going out before she went shopping. My mind raced as I tried to remember. Mom had left, but I didn't remember hearing anything after she went out. Jake had waited until Mom left. He knew I was home alone. When I realized this, my body became stone cold, unfeeling except for fury; pushing me beyond fear, into an animalistic rage in my head.

From then on I watched him with wrath. Whether he was drunk or sober, I did what I could to avoid him as my hatred toward him grew. His visits to my bed weren't uncommon when he was drunk, but knowing he could hurt me when he was sober felt like termites scavenging inside my brain, chewing me alive.

I felt crazy.

Life became surreal. The laughter and games I had created to remain sane no longer subdued my anxiety. Nothing did. I started smoking cigarettes to calm myself and became preoccupied with stealing them, among other things.

After the bathroom intrusion, there was a shift in his behaviour. He wasn't as bold in his efforts to abuse me. It was as though he knew I was a mad dog willing to mutilate and kill if need be. My eyes vented rage when looking at him, and for a brief period he stopped coming to my bed, unless he was totally drunk and I was completely vulnerable, usually when I was asleep.

I turned up the volume of my already heightened intuition as I scanned his moods, carefully listening to his every move at night. The sounds of my sisters walking up the stairs to my bedroom were fast and quick. Jake's steps were heavy and slow as he tried to walk quietly. If I was fast enough, I could get in the hole in the wall when I heard him.

Held up in our house, I made my way to the hole in the wall where I talked to my imaginary host of spirits. I stashed cigarettes everywhere, and the hole in the wall became my smoking area. It wasn't unusual to find someone else hiding there too, so I made them smoke with me. Whether my sisters wanted to smoke cigarettes or not, we did.

In grade five I turned ten. Mom didn't hound me about school anymore. We were left to take care of ourselves most of the time anyway. My sisters did well in school; they looked forward to going so they could play with their friends.

Wish I wasn't ten with tired eyes and a tired mind. I'll cash in the bottles tomorrow and miss another day of school. Don't know if I'm hungry or lonely. My stomach just gets smaller, and I'm finding it harder to breathe stale air that smells like the party they left behind. It's been three days since we were left alone, but it hurts more when he's home cuz my skin peels when he touches me. Wish I wasn't ten with tired eyes and a tired mind.

INTERLUDE OF A CHILD

Jake remained in our lives. His behaviour was unpredictable, but we expected the unexpected. If not for the familiarity of insanity, and not knowing anything else, in time Jake became the father we never knew. He grew on us like a malignant cyst, and whether we liked it or not, he wasn't going anywhere. My sisters seemed to like him; at least they appeared to get along with him. I waged war, which only fuelled Mom's accusations that I was too sensitive and emotional.

There wasn't anything my sisters and I couldn't survive. We held each other together. Our fights determined our pecking order; whoever won was in control when we were left alone, but sometimes the fights were over not wanting the responsibility.

Between the ages of nine and eleven I lost track of people, places and events. Besides Mom, Jake and Dad, we periodically lived with Grandpa Jonas in Fort Chip or ended up at another relative's home when Mom tried to leave Jake, during which time my memory lapsed. Then there were visits to Uranium City to visit my grandparents too.

There are events I can't remember, other people who sexually abused me. The violence, abandonment and insanity of complete instability took its toll. I can place some things in order of my age, but for the most part, my mind is a jigsaw puzzle of pictures, pitfalls of traumatic traps resurrected from the nightmares of my psyche, an archive filled with years of moving back and forth between Fort Chipewyan, Uranium City and Edmonton.

The world spun with time, I danced into my fantasy world without knowing, falling into an abyss of incest, tasting decadent death wishes, dreaming of love's embrace, a child so sweet – their treat. How many desserts did I serve to a world of perverts who delighted in the innocence of a baby's ice cream. Am I a chocolate cake or hot cocoa for your cinnamon stick? What flavour am I tonight?

The moves, nonetheless, carried me through, with hopes of better things to come.

Jake was rarely if ever employed; he reaped the benefits of living off Mom and her welfare cheques. Being unemployed must have gotten to him, and being the bush man he was, they started returning to Fort Chipewyan to make a living on his trapline.

Leaving Edmonton to return to Fort Chipewyan was a welcome transition from city life. In the bush, seeing my grandparents alleviated the terror because Grandpa Jonas didn't tolerate Jake hitting Mom. Jake was on good behaviour, more often than not, around Grandpa.

In Fort Chipewyan, I was removed from my sisters and returned to Aunt Angeline and Granny Iyas for a short time, with my sister Ruth. I lived with them most of the school year. I think I was eleven.

Charting where I lived is determined by the houses I lived in. During these times, Mom attempted to leave Jake, which meant living out of a suitcase and landing on just about anyone's doorstep. Mom's choices of escape were usually her friends. The only problem was that she never knew what to do with all of us girls, so in the process, we ended up anywhere she could place us.

Mom's saving grace remained Grandpa Jonas. He was the one person she could count on.

In Fort Chipewyan, most everyone knew me, and if someone didn't, they would ask, "Who's your mom?" I'd tell them, and then they would place me: "Ohhh... you're Jonas's grand-daughter," or "You're one of Ann's girls."

Grandma Annie had passed on and now Grandpa Jonas lived in the old folks' duplexes in town instead of in Dog Head in the bush tent I so fondly remembered. The duplex had a furnace and electricity, which was progress from a wood stove. All the old folks' duplexes were built the same. The front porch opened onto the kitchen and living room, which had a large window and a vast view of Lake Athabasca. Down the hall from the living room were two bedrooms and the bathroom, where the wringer washer was stored. We took sponge baths in a tub and washed in a basin. I found I could breathe easier living with Grandpa.

In one of the bedrooms there was the back door, which led to our clothesline outside. The basement was used for storage, and there Uncle Lance kept a large plastic garbage pail where they made home-made raisin brew. There was also a window wide enough for us to sneak in and out of in the basement; Grandpa Jonas didn't like us girls staying out late so we found alternative routes to come and go.

Local people didn't have running water yet, but we had old Leo and his horses. Leo hauled water for a couple dollars a barrel. Or we hauled water ourselves, two pails at a time, from the water treatment plant about a kilometre behind the old folks' duplexes.

It took half a barrel of water to do laundry in the wringer washer. Dishwater drained into a slop pail underneath the kitchen sink, and we had a honey bucket in the bathroom for a toilet. Both had to be emptied every day.

Life was simple and safe with Grandpa Jonas. His displays of affection toward us were entertaining, with jump-start jigs and obscure "who done it" games. He enjoyed making us laugh. Grandpa Jonas's love shone upon us every day, easing our tired minds with his presence and warming our hearts with his laughter.

He woke at dawn, brewed tea, always with a cigarette dangling from his mouth, and then sat in his chair on the front step to watch the sunrise. Then he meandered to the Hudson's Bay store to join the oldtimers, who arrived one by one and situated themselves on the wooden bench in front of the store. They told stories, joked around and greeted people passing.

This was his daily routine.

Grandpa Jonas understood and spoke English, Cree and French. Most elders were bilingual, but Grandpa Jonas refused to speak English, only speaking in Chipewyan.

Aunt Angeline's house smelled of smoked moose hide, firewood, granny's Jergen's hand lotion and Vick's Vapourub. I could walk from Aunt Angeline's to Grandpa Jonas's duplex in a minute.

Granny Iyas didn't have the vigour she once had. She appeared frail, like a ripe pear gone soft, yet her voice still commanded attention. I'd often notice her looking in my direction as though she were intuitively reading me. I adored her and felt calm in her presence; her aura was peaceful in spite of her busyness as she scurried around the house as if the chores would never get done.

Granny Iyas would visit her sister, Aunty Celine. Granny Iyas kept me busy too, and when there was time on our side, Granny taught me how to bead and was patient with me, stroking my hair with her soft wrinkled hands; encouraging me to do my best.

Although she was now blind, she was skilled at the art of beading. I helped her separate the colours she would use. I marvelled at her steady pace, picking up a tiny bead with a sliver-sized needle head, and spinning links into a chain. It took her seconds to form several strands on her rope necklace, compared to my two- and three-bead pace.

Our time alone embraced me with a silent understanding. She knew I needed to be cradled in her love. I needed to feel special. When we were alone she'd send me to the Bay for treats; Bugles and pop were her favourites. Or she'd make her way to her bedroom, hunched over, cane in hand. She'd hide pemmican in the oddest places, in between her mattresses or in an old suitcase. She'd search her room until she found what she was looking for; it was usually in a crumpled brown bag. Granny was gracious when setting this treat for us, arranging the lard, bannock, jam and tea at the table, then telling me to sit and eat; then we'd have a good chew together.

School in Fort Chipewyan wasn't any easier. I thought the playgrounds in Edmonton were tough, but the kids here were brutal and travelled in packs. I fought every day or I'd be running a marathon home. When I was too scared to leave the school, I'd visit Sister Brady and she'd tell me stories of how smart Mom was and how well she had done in school.

My teacher took me under her wing and let me visit with her after school. She took it upon herself to show me proper table manners. I liked her. She taught me how to make pies, and I helped cook our meals. Sister Brady and my teacher knew I was being harassed and didn't mind my waiting until it was safe for me to walk home.

Most mornings I hid on the hill out back of Aunty Angeline's until she left for work and then I'd stay home with Granny, and she'd let me. It seemed she always knew when I needed this time alone with her. Living in Fort Chipewyan was another battlefield, only now there were more enemies than friends, and my sisters weren't always around to defend me.

Most of the time Granny Iyas spoke to me in Chipewyan, but she understood when I spoke to her in English, and I was able to interpret her gestures and broken English. I just nodded my head like I understood, sometimes making her laugh. I loved listening to her speak Chipewyan. Her voice brought me back to a place when I felt innocent and clean, a time not so long ago, yet it felt like an eternity.

We'd lived in a bush tent in Dog Head with Grandpa Jonas and our family then; I was three years old playing in the hills, running through a field of tall grass on my way to the mission school playground. At night, I was safely wrapped in a feather robe blanket, nestled close to whomever I had to share space with while the wood stove crackled fire and the voices of my grandparents lulled me asleep.

The only road in Fort Chipewyan that was paved was the airport road. Otherwise the roads were gravel, and most roads had a name. We lived on Sesame Street, or "Down the Road," the "road" being the airport road. Then there was "Up the Road," Bannock and Lard Avenues, Shot Gun Alley and Dog Head, or so-and-so's house if the road didn't have a name.

All of the children who lived with their grandparents in the old folks' home on Sesame Street fought, played and discovered puberty together. Depending on the family, parents, uncles, aunts, brothers and sisters could be living with one of the old folks. On both sides of Grandpa's duplex, half a dozen kids lived with their grandparents, and we were smack in the middle of about forty kids in the whole complex. Our area of town accounted for another fifty or more kids, and then there were cousins who'd visit.

On a hot day, we gathered for escapades at the dock for swimming, and at night we played tag in a field of grass or chased old Leo's horses. My favourite game was harassing the local RCMP into chasing us, and then we'd hide. The RCMP thought they'd pulled one over on us when the town set a curfew, which only made annoying them late at night more exciting.

Being in a small town surrounded by bush, we parachuted from birch trees, built forts and played tag, hide and seek and anything else we could make up. My older sister Sara and I formed a truce; having adults around who were capable of caring for us lightened our anger toward each other, to the point where Sara began allowing me to tag along with her and her friends. We'd pile into a wrecked car in the back of our cousin Jenny's house and smoke cigarettes. Then they'd wait for me to begin whispering stories late into the night as we curled up with each other in the back seat. Night after night we escaped into the lives of heroines and slain villains. Like a wizard, I beckoned gypsies, tyrants, little people, children and ghosts. All my fantasies came to life as I visualized courageous characters on fantastic adventures. My audience hung on my every word as I offered hope and love with endless twists of fate and triumph.

Soon my nights and days became preoccupied with another interest, named Adam. He was the boy next door who liked me, and I liked him. One night he stole a blanket from his granny's clothesline and we ran up the hill, trekked into deep bush, and made a bed beneath the stars. We held hands, practised kissing, and I received my first bona fide hickey. We feel asleep and were rudely awakened at five in the morning. It seems we hadn't gone as far back in the bush as we'd thought; in fact, we were lying on a hillside by the road. Uncle Lance woke us. He was not impressed, especially with my hickey, but the other kids were.

In Fort Chip we enjoyed a healthier diet of wild meat from the trapline or when Jake hunted. Moose, caribou, fish and grouse put colour back in our cheeks and meat on our bones again. Tania didn't like wild meat so Mom tricked her by telling her she was eating chicken when she was eating rabbit. My sisters and I held muskrat- and rabbit-skinning contests, enjoying smoked muskrat and boiled potatoes, or rabbit-porridge stew. A few families would travel by boat to Goose Island to camp. Life on the land at night was still and quiet as the moon lured waves ashore on a calm night, with gusty winds on a stormy night. In the distance, wolves howled, and by dawn, loons sang their love songs.

Listening to my sisters' laughter as we played on the beach and swam in the lake made every day last longer. The bush was the only place I felt safe, like I had lived there all my life. I didn't feel alone in the world, or lonely. Jake wasn't as mad or scary in the bush. He was more himself when he wasn't drinking.

He decided to take us camping at Jackfish Lake. Jake and Mom were drinking, which they continued in his boat, arguing all the way, when Jake suddenly jumped up. He grabbed his shotgun, yelling at Mom to steer the motor. Almost capsizing us, he aimed his gun toward an island. I accidentally moved the boat when he took a shot, and he missed a bear. Jake was enraged as he pushed Mom aside, grabbing the motor from her. I was happy he'd missed his shot. I had a special kinship with bears.

We didn't make it to Jackfish Lake. Instead, Jake landed the boat on an island. We damn near froze that night. He was still mad about missing his shot, and he said we needed to learn to live like Indians, and sleeping on the ground without a tent in freezing rain was how he intended to make us tough. Jake's boot camp became a four-day drunk as we girls and Mom tried to fend for ourselves with what little rations they had remembered to pack.

Living with Grandpa Jonas became crowded, so Mom and Jake moved into a trailer Up the Road, where we girls were bullied because we were the city chicks, or apples: red on the outside and white on the inside.

The trailer had three bedrooms and bathroom on one end; the living room, kitchen and dining room on the other end, near the entrance. Behind the trailer was the graveyard. Alongside us was another trailer, which was pretty much the same as ours. Along our main road were typical Indian Affairs housing and a few more trailers. The tin house left me feeling like a lost spirit wishing to return to the graveyard we lived beside.

Being left alone while we lived in Fort Chip wasn't as lonely as the city because there was always someplace to go and something to do. If Mom and Jake were partying or visiting, we took over the trailer and played Creedence Clearwater full on while other kids in the area came over, sometimes – especially when we first moved there – to beat the hell out of us.

Most of the families still trapped, and, like Mom and Jake, other parents partied too. Not all of the neighbours drank, but the ones who did were much like ours when it came to kids fending for themselves. It was the most normal neighbourhood, yet because several families' lives resembled ours, it seemed we weren't the only kids with parents who drank and fought.

We girls were old enough to take up baking, and we took turns cooking. Grandpa Jonas had an account at the Bay, which we used when we needed to, until we'd racked up his grocery bill beyond his means. We listened to music and generally enjoyed ourselves when the storm calmed between Mom and Jake's drinking bouts.

The differences between living in Edmonton and Fort Chipewyan were obvious and simple, and if there was any consolation to living in Fort Chip, it was having relatives to turn to. I still hadn't told anyone what Jake did. We remained poor and always hungry; especially since moving away from Grandpa Jonas, yet there was always money to buy bootleg booze.

My sisters and I made our own way, spending time with friends and relatives. For me, it seemed I was either hiding at home from bullies, or running away from home to hide from Jake. We girls became scattered, and the tightknit family we once knew as little girls was slowly ripping apart as we grew older. Sara spent most of her time with her friends, as did Carol. Bobbie remained close to home, as did my younger sisters. It was a tag team between my older sister and me; whoever found herself at home alone with my younger sisters was the one left babysitting.

I wanted to have a party for my twelfth birthday. Mom said no, she was broke, and then later in the day she gave me a pack of cigarettes and twenty dollars. They were drinking and I guess she figured it was time I stopped stealing her cigarettes and hiding my habit.

The jukebox at Mah's Café rocked every night with the Eagles, Rod Stewart and other seventies and eighties bands. Most nights ended at the café, passing time away from home. It seemed that everyone wanted to take a round out of me, and survival meant fighting. Hell, everywhere we'd lived I'd had to defend myself. That or take a good licking, so I'd learned to fight back, or run fast, depending on how many there were.

It was while we lived in this trailer that Jake's violence reached a psychotic level. Although Mom remained his main opponent in the ring, he now attacked and beat my sisters and me; we became his sideshow of terrorism. One day, Jake had my sister Carol by the throat, choking her in a death grip, up against the wall, high off the floor. Dora and her friend walked in on time, diverting Jake's attention away from Carol, who fell to the floor gasping for breath, and then both sisters escaped.

Charges were laid, but that didn't discourage Jake.

He cornered me once in the porch, blocking me with his body. I huddled in a ball on the floor beneath him. In the second it took for him to clench his fist to hit me, I bolted underneath his arm and ran away. There were times I didn't think things could get worse, yet Jake proved me wrong.

I had discovered Nancy Drew when we lived in Edmonton. During my wanderings I came across a library near our house and started reading. I read whenever I could during the day; when it was safe to lie in bed.

One night I heard moans and someone's muffled whimper. I got out of bed and leaned against the door to listen. I froze when I heard Bobbie crying. Feeling her terror paralysed me. He was sexually abusing her, too. I shut out the sounds of her attempts to fight back. Not being able to help her felt worse than being abused myself. I curled up in bed and cried, waiting for him to finish. When he came out of the bedroom, Bobbie's sobs ripped me apart. I couldn't go to her. For the first time, I imagined ways of killing Jake.

The one thing I feared more than anything had happened. Determined not to allow it to happen again, I told Mom what I had heard Jake do, only to receive a sharp slap in the face.

I never said anything to Bobbie. The secrets that lingered within the tin walls of our trailer suffocated me. A sad heaviness weighed in my sister's eyes, overshadowing the sparkle she had. Swallowing our secrets constricted my throat, choking the life out of both of us.

Not being allowed to tell anyone what Jake did meant I could not protect my sisters, which distanced me from them. I stayed away from home and spent all of my time with friends and at Grandpa Jonas's. I decided to move out permanently, no matter what. I'd already left in my mind.

Mom moved back to Edmonton, fuelling my obsession to find Dad. The few times I had contacted him on the phone, I begged him to let me live with him and hounded Mom to send me to him.

Mom managed to convince Dad to send Sara, Carol and me to visit our grandparents on Dad's side of the family in Uranium City. During our visit with my grandparents in Uranium City, I gained weight. Both grandparents were professional cooks, and every day we devoured a feast of meat and potatoes and delicious desserts of pies, cakes, and Grandma's home-made donuts.

Grandma Isabelle wore a skirt and always had a sweater on, like Granny Iyas. She even wore moccasins like her. Grandma Isabelle kept me busy in the kitchen, teaching me how to bake and cook, or she had me run errands to the store for her. Each morning I blossomed in their security as the familiarity of their voices and movements in the kitchen reminded me I was safe.

One morning I felt sick with cramps and I had a headache. In the washroom I noticed my underwear was stained with blood. I told Grandma. She sent me to the store to buy pads and told me to read the package and wear the pads. The following five days I stayed at home feeling clumsy and awkward as my body changed; checking myself every hour in the bathroom, angry and frustrated with having to be conscious of the flow of blood.

Relieved when the bleeding stopped, I wanted to know when it would happen again. Grandma said in a month and every month after, for most of my life. She warned me, "Now you can have babies." She was stern in her tone and look. The thought scared me. I knew where babies came from and how a girl got pregnant, I just didn't know what having a baby had to do with me. I'd never let a boy have sex with me. Nervous of even the thought, I promised myself never to have sex until I wanted a baby.

After the change, I carried on exploring Uranium City and spending time with Grandpa Emile. He wore glasses and had brown eyes and his hair was greying. I found comfort in his company; he was kind-hearted, never raising his voice at us, even when he enjoyed a beer now and again.

My uncles took us fishing and cared for my sisters and me, seeing to it that we stayed out of trouble. I especially got along with Uncle Roger. He bought me a bike over the summer. I rode it to the hospital, where I volunteered as a candy striper once a week. I enjoyed helping the nurses with patients for two months during summer.

Grandpa Emile often brought me along with him when he worked on a traditional skiff he was building by hand. He told me stories of how he'd learned to build these boats when he was a young fisherman. He walked with a cane and had a limp from an injury at the mission, but he managed to manoeuvre around effortlessly nonetheless.

Most nights there was a card game going on in their basement, usually poker. My sisters and I were allowed to watch. It was fun listening to the players tell stories or tease each other, and yet be intensely involved in a serious poker game all at the same time. Grandma Isabelle held her own game too.

Sara was out with her friends most of the time. Carol and I stayed home more often. Though we had a curfew, I didn't mind. I knew what to expect when living with Grandma Isabelle from visiting her when we were younger. She was old fashioned in her ways, and her strict demeanour kept me in line; having a schedule and rules to adhere to was comforting because of the stability.

We made friends too. Angel and Bev lived across the back alley from us. They were sisters. I spent most of my time with them and tried to relax enough to be a kid. They were regular girls, which made me self-conscious, so I tried to play the role, behaving like I hadn't seen the things I'd seen or done the things I'd done. We did girl stuff, taking walks, giggling, and having fun on sleepy sunny days near the river. I'd always been a tomboy, yet in their company, it was okay to do girly things. Still, I remained sceptical and paranoid of everyone, and became a bully if someone poked fun at me; I was ready to throttle them. Now and again I would mention something about my life with Mom, bragging about my sisters or my escapades of thievery. Angel and Bev listened with empathy when I flippantly referred to Jake's violence like it was nothing, which usually shocked them, so I decided not to say much and pretend like I didn't know what I knew.

Angel and Bev hadn't seen much hardship, at least not like I'd known. I couldn't relate to their lives any more than they could relate to mine. I viewed them as fragile. I began to realize that I had experienced more than a girl my age should when it came to most everything. I knew that I'd never have what they had: the comfort of enjoying the freedom that came with having parents who offered the security of a safe home. I envied and admired them as we enjoyed the simple joys of being in a small town, savouring our time, dreaming, laughing and talking silly boy talk.

I didn't know how to be a prissy girl, and though Grandma encouraged me to take care of myself and my appearance, I was content with a good pair of running shoes and clean underwear. Most of the clothes I had when I first arrived at Grandma's no longer fit because I was growing and gained weight overnight. By the end of the summer, I was a plump fifteen pounds heavier and didn't feel comfortable with how I looked.

My sister Sara became close friends with our cousin, and they managed to get themselves into mischief, yet in everyone's eyes, my cousin was perfect and incapable of doing anything wrong, so Sara usually got blamed. Grandma often compared me to my cousin, telling me I should dress like her, fix my hair like her, and behave more like a lady, like her. One day I stormed out of the house yelling at Grandma that I wasn't my cousin, surprising her with my reaction. She never compared me to her again.

LOST CHILD

After the summer with my grandparents in Uranium City, we were sent back to Fort Chipewyan, where Mom and Jake still lived in the trailer. Mom and Jake continued going back and forth between Edmonton and Fort Chipewyan seasonally, and our lives remained much the same. Grandpa Jonas was happy when we came home to visit him, and when we weren't there his heart was burdened with loneliness for his kids. I remained with Mom for the winter, after which she moved back to Edmonton in the spring. It had been a long winter, and I was happy when once again Sara, Carol and I returned to Uranium City for the summer.

Over the summer in Uranium City, I had met Harry. He was nineteen and I was twelve. I couldn't believe someone older than me, especially someone as popular as Harry, could be interested in me. I'd seen him around town, and when he asked me to go for walks or have coffee at the hotel restaurant, I gladly accepted. I knew older girls his age liked him, so I felt special when he made time for me.

Tickled with infatuation, I told my girlfriend Debbie that Harry and I were going out. She stumped me when she asked if I had had sex with Harry yet. The idea terrified me, and when I told her that I had never had sex with anyone, she laughed at me and teased me for being a virgin, bragging that she wasn't. The thought of anyone touching my body reminded me of what Jake and the others did, which was something I didn't want to think about. As she taunted me, I got mad and pushed her. She wanted to fight, but the shame and embarrassment I felt from our conversation immobilized me, so I walked away.

My body changed over the summer, and I reluctantly changed too. The feelings I had for Harry confused me. I wanted him to hold me, to kiss me. I liked the way he looked at me, the way he talked to me, like I was important. What I didn't like was the way I looked. I'd always felt ugly, and for the first time how I looked mattered to me. I took time to comb my hair and dress nicely, and obsessed over my teeth, brushing them several times a day.

Harry took notice of my efforts to groom myself, and that was all the attention I needed. He made my tummy flutter and brought out a shyness I didn't know I had. It felt awkward; I was always so bold and forthright, but around Harry, my ability to think and speak left me. I did manage to stammer out a few words: where I was from, who I was and what I was doing there. Over time, I got over my shyness around Harry, and when I did, he liked me nonetheless. No matter how I felt about myself, he made me feel pretty and okay to be me.

Between the giggly-girly times at the beach, gossip-gabbing coffee times with my friends at the hotel restaurant, and groups of us walking around town for no reason other than to hang out, Harry was never far away. I remained the tomboy I'd always been, yet something was different. I still swore too much and delivered a fast right hook if annoyed or teased, yet there was enough downtime to relax and be a teenager without having to worry about anything other than making it home in time. I let my guard down enough to enjoy life, and made time to be alone where I retreated to my special place.

Hundreds of kilometres of bush surround the isolated town of Uranium City. The only road in and out of town was the winter road. It was the same in Fort Chipewyan. The towns were at opposite ends of Lake Athabasca. Uranium City is snuggled near the east shore, and Fort Chip along the west shore. In the bush and near the lake, I felt embraced by the familiarity of the land.

About a kilometre out of Uranium City, on the road to Eldorado, beneath a small bridge, a stream filtred over a subtle waterfall, which flowed into the lake five kilometres down river. By the waterfall, a favourite meditative spot for me, I spent a lot of time listening to the water caress the shoulders of the shoreline, gliding over rocks as the stream collected twigs and branches, clearing debris along its path before being swallowed by the lake.

While sitting along this embankment, I drifted into dreams of being surrounded by fairies and spirits who watched over and protected me. I felt blessed, leaving me giddy with laughter and feeling as light as a pixie. It was easy to cross over into an imaginary wonderland while the stream absorbed my sadness like a sponge as the water calmly sang to my spirit, if ever so briefly sedating my restlessness.

In my solitude, I allowed my troubles to float by, and for what seemed like the first time in my life, I was reprieved of memories that haunted me. The soothing flow of the water calmed me enough to afford me peace of mind. This carried me through a summer of all-consuming puppy love before we had to return to Mom in Edmonton.

I landed in Edmonton like a meteorite crashing from another planet.

We lived near the drag again, on 107 Avenue and 95 Street. I had no friends there, so I would crawl out of the living room window and watch the neighbourhood as I sat atop the porch roof of our brown, two-storey stucco house.

Harry had told me he was going to Edmonton to visit his mom and sister, and knowing this had made going back easier. Harry had told me when he was arriving before I left Uranium City and had given me his phone number. The moment he was supposed to be in, I phoned him. He invited me to his place, where we ordered Chinese food and rented movies.

I got along with his sister, and their mom didn't seem to mind me being there, so every chance I had, I went to Harry's. If I wasn't at Harry's, I hung around the rollerdrome or at a teen nightclub, despite pimps who tried to solicit me.

While trolling the city and our neighbourhood, I met a gang who tried to coerce me into joining them. I didn't want to. It became a game of avoidance and watching out for them from atop the porch roof. All I wanted to do was spend time with Harry, but when he became sexually aggressive, he frightened me. I didn't know how to react when he tried to have sex with me. It hurt. I'd end up crying while I lay stiff. Yet his efforts didn't discourage me from seeing him because he filled a void and fed me. Spending time with him was a better option than being at home.

Jake took notice of my curvaceous body and breasts that blossomed over night. There was a hunger in his eyes I knew too well, and he went further and further every time he came to my bed. I detached myself from my body altogether when the abuse was occurring. In the past, he never went farther than removing my underclothes, but now he tried to take all my clothes off. I knew it was only a matter of time before he would rape me, and there wasn't anything I could do.

During the day, I was at war with him. I became fearlessly aggressive whenever he attempted to get close or talk to me. I told him off with total disregard for any consequences. Whether he was drunk or sober, I reacted to him with a spiteful vengeance and sliced him with my words. I kept my secret to myself when my sisters or Mom reprimanded me for being angry all the time, enraged and frustrated that no one knew and I couldn't tell them.

I started to wear make-up and to dress in clothes that made me look older than I was. No one knew my age. I didn't act like a twelve year old and I didn't feel like a twelve year old, and I wasn't treated my age either. Mom and her friends talked to me like an adult, about adult things. They thought nothing of joking about their sexual encounters, or telling me their problems or who their latest boyfriends were. When I babysat for them, there was no regard for my time when they went out, often staying out for days while leaving me with their kids.

I behaved like an adult too. I didn't know any other way to be myself. I smoked cigarettes openly, bummed cigarettes, and wondered where the next meal was coming from. Hiding from Jake when he was drunk was the only thing I obsessed over. The violence had long since become old news; all we knew was to protect Mom from Jake when he beat her.

Otherwise, I was preoccupied with going out, or being with Harry. I remained insecure and self-conscious about my appearance, and the only clothes I owned were clothes I shoplifted, or anything I might have been able to guilt Mom into buying for me when she got her welfare cheque. I rarely came by what I owned honestly, without conning someone.

The trick was salvaging what wardrobe I had from the scavengers who raided it. Mom's friends frequently walked off in my jeans, or wore one of my shirts, like my wardrobe was a second-hand store. Between my sisters and me, we recycled clothes, which was fair game most of the time. I did laundry at the corner laundromat, and once had a complete load of laundry stolen from a dryer. There was a known flop house to the right of the laundromat, three buildings over. I intuitively knew to search for my laundry there. I was greeted at the door by a girl who was wearing my white-patched jeans, which I told her to remove or I would phone the police after I'd kicked the shit out of her. She gave my belongings back to me while explaining that her room-mate, who wasn't home then, had told her she'd found the clothes at a used clothes bin at the Sally Ann. I ignored her lies, grateful to have what little I owned back.

Our house was becoming an estrogen-soaked wasp's nest as we older girls matured, guaranteeing a sharp bite when agitated during our moon time. If not for our ability to find humour in anything, we would have stung each other to death.

At home, I shifted between taking care of my sisters and looking out for myself when I couldn't handle the responsibility. My younger sisters waited with open beaks to be fed and cared for.

I became claustrophobic when I had no privacy or personal space, so I left my troubles at home. The streets were safer. Jake slowly began to change his attitude towards me, and I knew if he didn't come to my bed, another sister was at risk of abuse. I listened to his every movement in the middle of the night, storming in on him any time he tried to bother us, even if it meant a beating.

If the police weren't at our door, the fire department was.

Our neighbour downstairs, Crazy Cassie we called her, was once married to a fireman, and when she got drunk she'd phone the fire department, or had one of us kids phone them. Then she would lie naked on her couch, waiting for them to arrive. One day she actually caused a fire and blamed Mom, creating a feud that lasted a couple of weeks. The fire was put out before any serious damage occurred, but it left Cassie living in smoke and ashes.

Then, on my thirteenth birthday, Harry invited me over, telling me he wanted to celebrate with me, that he had something special for me. Excited, I dressed as best I could, applied my dark blue eye shadow, and caught the bus to his place. When I arrived, he offered me a drink of lemon gin. It burned when I swallowed it, and it made me dizzy. Harry and his sister laughed when I told them how dizzy

I felt. They poured me another glass, coaxing me to guzzle the drink. I wanted to throw up, but they poured me another, which I did throw up, barely making it to the toilet in time.

I couldn't walk straight, so Harry told me to go to his bedroom, and while I lay in his bed the room started to spin. Harry crawled in with me. I couldn't stop him as he quickly tore off my shirt and pulled it over my head, unzipping my pants and pulling them off too. I started to cry, telling him to stop, but before I could do anything, he was on top of me. He spread my legs and plunged himself into me, pushing himself in and out. I felt something rip inside while I bled in agonizing pain. When Harry stopped, he got up and dressed himself. He threw my clothes at me and told me to get dressed and go home. Stunned, bleeding, and sore, I cried as I dressed myself while begging him to let me stay. He started yelling at me to get the fuck out and told me not come back or bother him again. I followed him into the living room. His sister sat on the couch laughing. When I wouldn't leave, he pushed me out the door and said he would phone the police if I didn't leave him alone.

Sobbing and drunk, I noticed my jeans were bloody as I staggered to a bus stop. I managed to find my way home on the bus, where I wandered around our neighbourhood for what felt like hours, too fearful to face Mom. I eventually got cold and almost passed out on the street so I sneaked in and changed my clothes before crashing in my bed.

The next day, I couldn't face Mom when I remembered what had happened. Once again I wanted to tell someone, but there was no one I could talk to, there was nothing I could do. All I could think about was Harry telling me he didn't want to see me again. I thought he must have been too drunk to know what he was doing or saying. Maybe he was joking – maybe he was afraid his mom would come home and he didn't want her to catch me in his bed. Hundreds of thoughts raced through my mind, and in a panic, I went to his house. He refused to talk to me. For days I continued trying to see him, and each time I was told to leave him alone.

My sanctuary had been a trap, and I couldn't handle rejection from the only person I trusted. I started drinking wherever and whenever I found a party at the rollerdrome or teen club.

Lost in a strobe light fantasy, shaking my hips, grinding my bones, grooving to bass tones, trembling to forget home as I flashdance into your imagination, I can be who you want me to be cuz, Harry, he don't want me anymore, so set me free in a bottle, we'll escape on a dance floor, where my body is mine to move, just don't end the night cuz I'm running away from the troubles of a street child...

Every time I got drunk, I attempted to see Harry. I stalked him and followed him to a party where I was threatened by someone he knew: either I leave him alone or she'd slap me out. I was thrown out of the party. I staggered down the street while I listened to their jeering as they laughed at me.

I discovered I couldn't feel when I was drunk, so I got drunk as often as I could, until the craving to drink consumed me. It was easy to steal booze at home. I was beyond caring about anything or anyone, as I found myself searching the neighbourhood for escape.

Two blocks from our house, I met Frank. He lived with his kokum. I wanted his approval and acceptance. It was clear what he wanted, and I needed to be held. In Frank's arms, I became a trusting child.

We kept meeting until his kokum found us naked in the tiny storage room where he would take me. She was screaming at Frank in Cree, hitting him with her cane while I got dressed. She kept screaming at Frank that he was twenty-one and I was only a girl. She called him a pig. I wasn't allowed to go back to Frank's, and during my wanderings in the neighbourhood, the gang finally caught up with me. I managed to escape without getting beat up.

I was unwilling to stay at home or walk the neighbourhood any more. I tried to contact Dad, but he was on the road. I didn't go to school, I just hung out, aimlessly going through each day without direction. I fell into another deep depression, which was briefly subdued when I drank. Every day became a quest to escape reality, until I met up with Samantha.

We knew each other from Uranium City, and when I ran into her at the teen nightclub in Edmonton, we started hanging out. Sam was into vogue fashion and took her preppy persona seriously. When she did hang out with me, it was usually because I could find a drink easier than she. I knew who to talk to, and the pimps were more than willing to provide me with alcohol. They offered me drugs too, but I never accepted because I knew that was how they lured girls to work the streets for them. I hung out with whomever would provide me with a drink, then I stepped back when I got what I wanted.

Sam was Asian and beautiful. Neither of us looked our age. Sam was fourteen, and as tiny as she was, if she wore make-up, she easily passed for eighteen. I was introduced to Jennifer through Sam, and the three of us shared an appreciation for clothes and the art of shoplifting.

Jen was fourteen and lived with a foster family that she hated. There wasn't much Jen liked about anyone or anything, and I'd never met anyone with as much street savvy or attitude as she had. She was a brunette, with natural curls and big blue eyes she adorned with black eyeliner. When she walked into a room, everyone noticed.

Sam came from a wealthy family and vicariously lived her life through Jen and me. I never understood her need to fit in, especially when she couldn't relate to the frontline stories Jen and I swapped about life at home. I'd been talking about Crazy Cassie who lived beneath us one night when Jen freaked out and told me to shut the fuck up. Cassie was her mom. She was seven when she was apprehended by Social Services, and had been in foster care since. I never mentioned her again.

I told Jen and Sam what had happened with Harry, and then I heard myself tell them that I was pregnant. Immediately, my fantasy pregnancy became a reality, in my mind, as I explained my crisis to them. That's why I had to run away. That's why I needed them. I gave a convincing testimony of what could be while they eagerly listened. It didn't take much to talk them into running away.

There's an angel child growing in me, can't you see the baby's wings will be our saving grace, we can all be Mommies, we three will be this angel child's keepers, and together we'll live happily ever after in our new life. We'll be a happy family ever after...

I had had my period since being raped, yet the more we talked about raising *our* baby, the more I believed my lie as Jen, Sam, and I talked about raising the baby together. Our talks turned into late-night grandiose schemes of wonderful things yet to come while we planned our escape.

We agreed on when to meet at the bus depot on the night we ran away. I panhandled twenty dollars, and between the three of us, it was decided I should carry the switchblade. Sam and Jen said that if it came down to defending ourselves, I would be courageous, or crazy, enough to do whatever had to be done.

From the moment we stood on highway 16 heading wast, we were lucky with the truckers. None of us had ever been to Vancouver, nor did we know anyone there. I was excited as we made plans to find jobs and a place of our own; all the while I acted on cue with my fantasy pregnancy as I rehearsed my plans with Jen and Sam. They merely nodded their heads as I enthusiastically talked about what we could do for work, even if it meant washing dishes. As long as we stuck together, everything was going to be okay.

The last trucker we hitched a ride with bought us something to eat at a truck stop in Merritt, B.C., making Jen and Sam nervous with his questions, asking where we were from and how old we were. We lied. Jen said she was from Vancouver; Sam and I were returning with her for a visit. That's all. He stopped prying and drove us into Vancouver, dropping us off near a bus stop.

Vancouver's city lights intimidated me. The city was bigger than Edmonton, and I was scared of this foreign landscape of highways I didn't recognize. We agreed to catch a bus, any bus, and let the route determine our destination. Getting on the next bus, Jen asked the driver where downtown was; annoyed, he mumbled a series of buses to transfer on.

From a suburban area, the route became increasingly busier with traffic and urban activity until we came onto what appeared to be an area of Vancouver we thought was close enough to downtown. "Hastings Street," the bus driver yawned.

On Hastings Street, we found another bus depot and stored our packsacks in a locker before finding a restaurant. We had enough change to buy a plate of french fries with gravy and coke.

I'd felt a shift in their attitude toward me since we arrived but ignored it, thinking Jen was still pissed at me for unknowingly laughing at her mom. At the restaurant, they became boldly rude toward me. I became nervous and went to the washroom. In the washroom I realized I had started my period. Panicking, I returned to the table, telling them I had just miscarried the baby in the bathroom and that I was bleeding, suggesting I get to a hospital.

Clashing with reality, this ride is over little girl. You slipped too far into your fantasy and now you have to pay the troll tapping on your door. Come out, come out wherever you are. You've gone too far...

Jen and Sam rolled their eyes back and started laughing.

"Jolene, you're so fucked up! You're not pregnant!" Jen's words cut me.

They then told me of their plan. They were going to prostitute themselves and find a rich sugar daddy. I was either with them or not. When we left the restaurant, we returned to the bus depot, where I tried to talk them out of working the streets. We got into a fistfight when I refused to give them the key to our locker. They left me after a security guard opened the locker for them.

The only person I could think of phoning was Harry. He hung up on me when I told him where I was. I thought of Mom. I had told her I was going camping with some friends. She believed me, or maybe she was too drunk to care. Either way, she didn't have a phone, so there was no way of contacting her.

I calmed down enough to phone the police. I told them I was a runaway. Within minutes, a policeman picked me up and took me to a youth emergency shelter, where the policeman and a social worker interrogated me.

They wanted me to provide descriptions of Sam and Jen. I refused to, regardless of the horror stories the social worker told me. I couldn't rat them out. They sent me to the waiting area when I wouldn't cooperate. I didn't like the social worker's attitude toward me or to the other street kids, so when she called me back in her office I said, "There must have been a time you cared. I mean, it had to take you years to get educated to do this work. So, tell me what the fuck happened, cuz you sure don't act like you care anymore." She didn't say anything, just sat in her chair, stunned. I stood and walked out of her office.

As it turned out, Sam and Jen were placed on a Canada-wide missing persons list, and while I was with the social worker, they were being escorted in by the police. When Sam and Jen saw me, I was pegged a rat anyway.

We were all placed in a group home, where I ended up defending myself against both of them. The staff were only too happy to allow me to resolve our differences as I pleased because Jen and Sam were trouble from the moment they arrived. I beat up Sam before Jen attempted to rescue her. I threatened Jen, telling her I'd throw her out a window if she bothered me. I walked away satisfied that they'd leave me alone.

The next day we were scheduled to go on a tour of Stanley Park with the staff. I decided to stay behind. When they returned, Sam and Jen made a run for it. The staff didn't bother chasing after them; they phoned the police instead. Mom received a visit from the police forty-eight hours after I'd left. The police told her I was in a group home in Vancouver. They needed to know if she wanted me placed in a foster home or returned to her.

She wanted me home.

I was sent back to Edmonton on a train. Sam and Jen remained on the run. The social worker I had told off brought me to the train station. Before I got on the train she placed her hands on my shoulders and said, "Kid, you're going to make it." Any one of the staff could have taken me to the station but I guess she felt the need to. We hugged and I thanked her.

DRUG STORE BABY

When the train arrived in Edmonton, Jake met me at the CN station downtown. He warned me that Mom was angry. He asked me what had happened, not why I ran away. We both knew. He listened without interruption as I described what the mountains looked like while providing all the details of my adventure, as if it were a school field trip rather than an attempt to run away. We suspended our feud enough to find neutral ground. As much as Jake was incapable of being a father-figure, there were times his efforts were appreciated. This was one of those rare moments. He said he was proud I'd turned myself in and that he hoped to one day go to Vancouver himself.

At home, he defended me against Mom when she attempted to beat some sense into me. It was late when I unpacked my backpack and then tried to repent after Mom got mad. Restitution meant a thorough house cleaning, not just sweeping the floor or washing a pile of dirty dishes – this was going to take an overhaul.

There were two things Mom did when she got angry: a beating, or she made you clean the house like your life depended on a shiny floor. My sisters were in bed as I nervously swept the floor in the bedroom, relieved Jake was able to talk Mom into going to bed. I was so scared that I woke up my sisters so I could sweep and mop underneath the bed; no wrath compared to Mom's if you forgot to sweep underneath and behind furniture. Mom often referred to how she was made to clean every corner when she was in the mission, and it had to be done thoroughly, or else. Scrubbing hardwood floors on her knees with a steel brush was a form of punishment. She told us girls we didn't know what a good cleaning meant.

Yawning and surprised to see me back, my sisters obliged me; they knew Mom was on the warpath. When they asked what had happened, I told them I didn't want to talk about it, and asked them to move to the next bed so I could sweep under theirs. Lifting the bed, I found six baby mice and swept around them. I was satisfied my job was done after the floors reeked of Pinesol cleaner, and when the baby mice and my sisters were sound asleep again, I too curled up in bed and fell asleep.

After four days, Mom eventually spoke to me, but only when she had to. I don't know what hurt her more: my lying to her, or the shock of having the police tell her that I had run away.

The familiarity of Edmonton's streets swallowed me as I resumed my routine at the teen dance club. The neighbourhood gang found me again – unfortunately for them. I was devoid of fear, and I challenged the leader of their gang, Angel, to a fight. I had nothing to lose after the Vancouver road trip; I was cocky and I didn't care. The years of pent-up rage from having to constantly defend myself erupted in Angel's face as my fists and feet pounded her into the pavement, after which I asked if anyone else wanted to have a go at me. They looked at me like I'd lost my mind. Angel lay on the sidewalk bleeding and crying. They never bothered me again.

Living at home with my sisters, we became involved in what came naturally in our neighbourhood. Mom was losing what little control she had over us, especially me.

I eventually contacted Dad and begged him to take me away, just send me anywhere. I cried and pleaded with him to get me out of Edmonton; he agreed to send me to Uranium City to live with his cousin, Aunt Rose.

Between twelve and thirteen years old, I sifted like sand through the lives of relatives and friends as I tried to fit in. Loneliness was my only companion as I continued to fear and reject what I most wanted and needed, to be loved and accepted, not knowing what either felt like, ignorant of the simplicity and presence of kindness.

Aunt Rose's home wasn't any different – I didn't fit in despite how comfortable she tried to make me feel. Her daughter Ruth lived with her. Ruth was eighteen. I basically stayed out of their way as I awkwardly made an effort to adjust to their tidy lives and routine, but I knew I'd screw up because I wasn't a carbon copy of Ruth, who was a nice girl.

Ruth had a nice boyfriend, graduated from high school, had a nice job, wore nice clothes, and acted her age, which was fine if you came from the planet of the Pollyannas, whereas I related more to the planet of the apes. Aunt Rose and Ruth gently encouraged me not to act so grown up, to behave more like the child I was, which only left me confused as to how. So much normality left me dizzy and perplexed, so I opted for a "fuck it" attitude, and spent most of my time in my room, where I listened to Dr. Hook day and night, crawled out of bed when I pleased, and dropped in whenever I wanted, drunk or stoned.

Aunt Rose made sure I registered at school. I turned fourteen in grade seven. I resumed what was typical behaviour for me: partying. It didn't take long to find people to hang out with, and they were always older than I was.

My friend Cheryl had a friend who drove us around, usually back and forth between Eldorado and Uranium City. Cruising as loud music vibrated off the car windows, we smoked pot and drank beer. I knew more guys than girls because they could handle my bad-ass attitude. The guys my age were only friends, unlike the men who offered me drugs or alcohol while hoping to have sex with me, which when I was drunk happened more often than not.

I didn't explore my sexuality because I enjoyed sex. The payoff was booze or drugs. The only thing I liked about being with someone was being held. For a brief time, I felt loved. I hungered for the physical warmth of a body close to mine, regardless of what was done to my body. I wanted someone to hold me, no matter how much it hurt; I had long since learned to numb the pain. I didn't enjoy the act of sex. It gave me no pleasure: it was a fix, a drug, a need to be needed and wanted.

I open my legs as they enter, closing my eyes as moans subside in love-smitten climaxes with any man who needs to feel like one. Just hold me, and like a dove, by morning I'll fly to another and shape-shift into their desire. My blessings are as beautiful as your hunger and need to be human, an angel child in your dreams and a dove in your arms...

A free-spirited wild-child roaming the town, meeting strangers, I viewed the world with a carefree optimism, living life on my terms as I physically matured into a sexy size four and filled out in all the right places. I knew how to get what I wanted, and looking older than fourteen helped. It was the attention I sought, and that was what was noticed.

My friends didn't pay attention to my behaviour. Everyone was too busy partying, even if I was front page news. At school I tolerated the kids. Most girls were getting over playing with Barbie and Ken while I was getting over a hangover, which left little room for mutual interest, so I remained on the outside looking in. I couldn't be bothered with the boys. They were immature and got on my nerves. I was beyond holding hands and playing tag with someone I liked. I just wanted to get drunk, and kids my age, for the most part, couldn't relate.

I was eventually removed from grade seven, and then placed in a special education classroom for kids with emotional and behavioural problems. Being called to the principal's office several times for being stoned and physically and verbally assaulting other students nominated a seat just for me in no time. The kids in this class were troubled students like me, so we got along.

Placing me in a group of troubled students was like providing me with a warrant that permitted deviant delinquency, and of course, a route to more drugs, drugs I hadn't tried yet. It began with buying Gravol pills over the counter at the local drug store, which we managed to buy out a few times. Then I discovered other hallucinogenic drugs, and life at fourteen became one long acid trip. The people I partied with were of legal age, and most of them assumed I was too, especially the men, and when they found out I was only fourteen, they couldn't have cared less.

Aunt Rose got word of my reputation, and she couldn't wait until Dad moved back. We were both happy when he did. Dad and I got our own place, and I became his housekeeper and cooked our meals. We set ourselves up in our home, yet in spite of our effort to live together, it was anything but a typical father-daughter relationship. I wouldn't listen to Dad – I wouldn't listen to anyone, and my rebellion created more heartache than headaches on both our parts. My trust in him was destroyed on a road trip to British Columbia when a truck driver was parked on the side of the road. Dad suggested I introduce myself to this stranger, and then he suggested that I spend some time alone with him. I stared at him, shocked and in disbelief. He was serious. I said no.

From then on, I trusted no one. Determined to do what I wanted, I set my mind on living on my own, sooner rather than later. I eventually got kicked out of school and went to work at the hotel restaurant. The other option was moving back with Mom, so I didn't mind washing dishes. When I got over my anxiety of people, I served tables. This job lasted a couple of months.

My drinking increased and so did my drug use and promiscuity. I moved in with my girlfriend, Loretta, after Dad kicked me out. Loretta's dad kicked her out too, and our place became a party house. Loretta was fifteen, a year older than me. Her family had moved to Uranium City a year before we met. When we first met, Loretta couldn't stand me. I was loud, blunt and rude. Over time and pot, we got to know each other.

Dad decided to put me to work for him as a dispatcher. He owned a taxi company. I subsidized my drug habit living with Loretta; she sold drugs on the side. Eventually, coming down from acid trips turned into an obsession with suicide. In an effort to end my lethal head game, I limited my drugs of choice to marijuana, drinking and living for the next party.

One night, I blacked out and woke up naked. The going joke in the morning was how many guys had had turns on me. Shortly after the gang rape, I tried to commit suicide. A friend found me in his bathroom on the floor and then rushed me to the hospital. I was docile as the nurses made me drink gallons of apple juice before pumping my stomach. I hadn't taken as many pills as I needed to fulfil my death wish.

The next day, Dad came to the hospital to see me. He asked if I was proud of myself. I lay in bed thinking what the hell kind of question is that? My head pounded as he stared at me, bewildered. With contempt, he asked me, "How do you think this makes me look? Do you know how it feels when people talk about my daughter, the easiest slut in town?" I turned away without looking at him. I thought about what had happened at the party, and remembered the hours before the party...

I was in a bunkhouse in Eldorado, drinking with a couple of men who shared a room. Daryl and Peter supplied me with all the drugs I wanted, as well as alcohol, and I made myself available to either of them. It was an easy exchange, and neither of them cared if I slept with the other. In fact, they took turns. I was too stoned and drunk to care.

I told Daryl I was late for a period, he looked at me dumbfounded. Peter overheard me. They nervously glanced at each other; Daryl then asked me when I had started having periods. I told him. Peter responded angrily, "What the fuck do you mean you missed a period"?

I shrugged my shoulders as I lay naked in bed with Daryl.

"She's spent more time with you man. It's your problem," Peter stated to Daryl, who was getting dressed and telling me to do the same. Peter swore aloud, telling Daryl to get rid of me; he was going to take a shower. Daryl suggested that I leave. I asked if I could stay for the night; he said no.

It was after midnight as I staggered toward the highway in freezing snow. I wanted to end my life as I lay down in the ditch. Falling in and out of consciousness, I closed my eyes, hoping to fall asleep and never wake up. A taxi pulled over. I recognized the driver; he drove taxi for Dad. He stepped out of his taxi and asked me if I was okay, and then offered me a ride to town.

When I was released from the hospital, I was sent back to Mom in Edmonton.

Loretta decided to leave Uranium City too and travelled with me to Edmonton. Mom agreed to let her stay with us. Our plan was simple: we'd get a job, a place to live, and make a new start. The job we found was panhandling in a park downtown, collecting enough money to buy weed or sneak into bars. During one of our late-night escapades, we met a crazed man in a bar who stalked us and then later chased us along Jasper Avenue in our attempt to lose him. He was convinced Loretta was his girlfriend, and when he caught up with her, he twisted her arm behind her back and held a knife at her throat. I arrived in time with a stranger I had grabbed on the street. The following week, Loretta decided to hitchhike to British Columbia to look for work after Jake tried to have sex with her while she was sleeping.

I stayed behind with a boyfriend until Loretta phoned. She'd found work in Blue River. I asked if I could join her. She reluctantly agreed – she knew what it was like at home living with Jake. I didn't want to stay in Edmonton, where I basically lived on the streets with the people I'd met, and I didn't want to return to Mom's. I took the bus to Blue River, where Loretta and I worked for another week before deciding to move to Kamloops, where Loretta's mom lived.

Sandra, Loretta's mom, said she couldn't afford to keep me after a few weeks. I was underage and unable to find work or receive social assistance without Sandra becoming involved with Social Services, and she didn't want to. Loretta told me she wanted to work things out with her family. I didn't realize I was the problem.

Her parents had separated years ago, and Sandra knew Loretta's father had kicked her out of his home when she was living with him in Uranium City. He also warned Sandra about me, and then forbade Loretta to have anything to do with me, which is why he had kicked her out in the first place. He refused to have anything to do with her afterward.

I told Loretta I understood when she explained her situation to me.

Loretta then confided something else to me. She passed me a note from beneath the bathroom door and asked me to read it. As I read the note, I felt sick. When she came out of the bathroom, we cried in each other's arms. Loretta had been raped, and we both knew who raped her. She was afraid I would hate her for telling the truth. I understood she needed to talk about what had happened. I assured her it wasn't her fault and told her how sorry I was for what had happened to her.

We sealed our secrets in friendship and said our good-byes.

When I returned to Edmonton, I knew I couldn't live with Mom and Jake without getting into serious trouble, so I made plans to move back to Uranium City. I contacted a couple I'd met after I managed to line up a job as a cook's helper in a bush camp through a friend who worked for a mining company. Nadine and Rick agreed to allow me to room with them, and in exchange, I would babysit until I was able to save enough money to pay rent. They knew I was only fourteen.

Dad paid for my plane ticket when I told him I had a job and a place to live. Once in Uranium City, my living arrangements lasted only a couple of months over the summer. Nadine and Rick were going through their own personal struggles, constantly fighting, and they told me they didn't need the hassle of all the tomcats wailing outside their door late at night looking for me.

When they asked me to move, I found other places to stay, after another attempt to live with Dad and his girlfriend failed. Living in a small town, crashing out with friends got me by, most of the time.

Lost child so pretty and free, won't you come home with me, I've got something to make you feel better, just lay down your tired soul and we'll go for a slow ride, marijuana baby let me touch your tender body, so young and sweet, we'll meet on a cloud tonight and I'll make everything all right. Spinning out of control, got nowhere to go so take it easy and slow...

I burned all my bridges with family after I rejected another relative's attempt to help. I remained homeless, and whenever anyone tried to intervene I refused to accept their help. Social Services apprehended me and placed me in a foster home; within a week, I was kicked out. The friends I moved in with couldn't handle my erratic moods and neurotic behaviour. I slept wherever

I could, tripping around town like a flower child. People called me crazy. Habit and survival birthed a seductress hidden behind a sunny disposition, which afforded me several male friends to shack up with when I had to. In exchange for a place to live, I offered sexual favours and the services of a cleaning lady.

I ignored the efforts of several people who tried to help me. I lost track of the men I'd been with. My spirit detached from my body with each lover, severing me from myself altogether until I couldn't stand to let a man touch me. I was left on the brink of total isolation and alienation. I walked barefoot for miles in the bush. I slipped into my surreal wonderland, away from people, returning to the only place I'd ever felt safe.

VISITED

I felt inclined to wear skirts, so I cut all my jeans inside the centre seam and patched them with any material I could, creating pretty-funky skirts. I didn't want to drink or use drugs, so I stopped. I felt a need to be alone, so I hiked between Eldorado and Uranium City, walking over twenty-five kilometres a day.

The road from Eldorado curved around a sharp bend, turning onto a view that displayed picturesque rolling hills flowing into a valley of red willow brush near Lake Athabasca's shoreline.

Cattails were silhouetted by tall grass swaying in ponds that filtered earth's roughage and debris. Nature's opera of crickets, frogs and ravens accompanied a string section of wind blowing through the trees. A calm tenor of waves lightly lapping equalized the squeals of seagulls diving for fish.

As I walked barefoot on asphalt, my body tingled with sensation. I closed my eyes to listen. Twelve metres away from me, to my right, a bear's heavy paws crunched twigs and leaves, slowly and intently manoeuvring toward me. She stopped, camouflaged behind dense bush and willow branches. I could hear her breathe. We stood still and listened to one another. I gave thanks for her presence. She sat still as I acknowledged her. Walking closer toward her, I sat on a large boulder awkwardly situated in the middle of nowhere, as though it had dropped out of the sky. I couldn't see her, yet sensed she was only a few metres away, huddled in bush.

I hummed a song for her and prayed. I then stood, as did she, and we walked away from each other. Her large frame momentarily stopped as a car drove by; we both shivered when the noisy metal roared past. I heard her growl a good-bye as she quickly dodged through thick bush.

I waited until I couldn't hear her move, lonely. A white bunny hopped up to my feet and scratched his nose before hopping away. I returned to the highway content to have been accompanied by a brother and sister of God's/Goddess's creation. I succumbed to an inner peace and calm. Alone but for miles of dense bush surrounding me, I sang to and spoke with my guides, tuning into waves of electrical currents dancing throughout the boreal forest. Every botanical organism quivered in life's essence, laughing and singing with me.

The shimmering of the lake's shore melted into earth, air, and sky. Sheer white clouds adorned the sun's illuminating rays. Sundogs leapt onto the horizon, greeting me with exhilarating rushes, showering me with spectacles of sunbeams, elevating my spirit as I felt the cosmos at the centre of my being reach out and engulf life's creation, until I became one with the universe.

From above, I witnessed a young girl smiling, her arms extended to the heavens. She was surrounded with golden lights blessing her spirit as her guides prayed around her, for her. The angels rejoiced in her communion with the Holy Spirit.

Gliding toward her, I looked closer and saw it was me walking as my highest self residing in my corporal body. Angels beckoned me to remain close so as not to disturb the initiation of crossing over.

I felt safe as I travelled amongst the angels guiding me, until all I felt were cascading ripples of love as I witnessed a child of Goddess/God. I became a bright light extending itself beyond my environment, connecting me with the universe. Instantaneously, angels carried me into the heavens as I walked in grace on earth, and for a fleeting moment, I travelled outside of my body with my guides.

Later, I found it difficult to be with people as their auras out-shone their physical being. I felt compelled to offer psychic read-ings of what I witnessed within their souls and around them. I startled most people with my accuracy, and they balked nervously when they saw me again.

I continued walking barefoot daily, seeking solitude. I walked in an other-worldly state, without concept of time or cerebral limitations; reality was intangible.

If I had to, I could sneak into one of the bunkhouses in Eldorado for a place to sleep. The recreation rooms had several couches, a television, tables with decks of cards and a cribbage board. If I arrived late enough, no one noticed. One evening, a resident nicknamed Shark found me curled up on a couch. I knew by his aura that he was dangerous. As I was about to leave, he said, "Don't worry, you can stay. I won't hurt you. I'm here to warn you." I sensed his intention was sincere so I listened. Keeping his distance so not to alarm me, he continued: "Tomorrow a coyote will pass in front of you. When this hap-pens, watch for an old man walking toward you. This old man will appear harmless, but he's dangerous, so don't go with him." As Shark spoke his face transformed; he was no longer a man: he was a beastly figure. He knew I could see his spirit-form but ignored my fears. "I won't harm you."

He started walking up the stairs. "You can sleep in my room if you want." I shook my head no. "Suit yourself, but I'm in 221 if you change your mind. I'd be careful if I were you – living in grace isn't all light. You'll see."

As he turned the corner, I could see that the bottom half of his body was hoofed like an animal and his face deformed. His eyes were demonic and his large head had two small horns covered in a thick mane of hair and animal fur. "Don't assume you're safe because you can sense... us. Sweet dreams."

He disappeared up the stairwell. I lay awake for as long as I could before falling asleep by morning light.

I woke at noon and realized how late it was. I knew security had already made their rounds and was surprised they hadn't bothered me. They would have seen me sleeping on the couch. I decided to hitchhike back to town rather than walk.

Standing by the road, a coyote crossed in front of me. It looked directly at me, stopped, and quickly turned away, disappearing in a hill off the road.

"Good afternoon!" someone yelled.

I looked down the hill. Walking toward me was an elderly man. I had a flash of myself bleeding and lying naked in the bush, dead. Before he got any closer, I ran as fast as I could toward the recreation complex at the bottom of the hill. He grunted as he tried to stop me, but I was too quick. Racing into the restaurant, I saw an elderly man I had befriended sitting alone.

Gasto had taken me under his wing one day when he found me wandering around the complex and had watched out for me ever since. I joined him at his table, and he looked at me with concern. "You look like you've seen a ghost." I was shaking. A waitress came by and asked if I wanted anything. Gasto ordered breakfast and coffee for me, smiling as he winked at me.

Shark came into the restaurant and saw me sitting with Gasto. He nodded his head in acknowledgement and then walked out. Gasto turned around when he saw the expression on my face. No one was there.

"Is everything okay?" I said yes. "If something is wrong you can talk to me." I nodded my head yes. "Well, okay. Just want you to know I'm here. Have you found a place to live yet?" Gasto tried not to interfere in my life, but he couldn't help but ask. I ignored his question.

I had had a place to live a few days ago. There were people who cared enough to allow me to stay with them periodically, particularly one girlfriend, Lorna. Lorna's family took me in for a couple weeks, until they became concerned with my influence on Lorna and she wasn't allowed to hang around me anymore.

After breakfast with Gasto, I waited in the restaurant until I found someone who was going back to town that I could catch a ride with. Gasto wasn't the only person watching out for me — some of my dad's friends kept an eye on me too.

I regressed further into myself as people welcomed me or shunned me. My age was of no consequence. I didn't feel fourteen. I didn't feel any particular age. I felt timeless and wholeheartedly sensed the presence of spirit guides protecting me, embracing my soul.

Leaving my body came naturally. I had honed the ability to exit my body when I was being sexually abused as a child. Opening a portal to my psyche, tuning my volume of heightened sensory perception enabled me to intuitively feel beyond the physical realm of existence, beyond facades and superficial pleasantries. Now I experienced people through the eyes of God/Goddess and my guides. People sought me out for readings, and I read palms, handwriting, and their minds, much to their discomfort. It was disconcerting for them to have a fourteen-year old girl view their soul. I witnessed each soul with a clarity that surpassed common sense and intuition, feeling and sensing the very core of a stranger's inhibitions, fears, dreams, desires, pain, love. Everything they experienced, I too felt, as if I were in their corporeal body.

Sometimes what I witnessed through the experience of others wasn't a good feeling. Unable to disassociate myself from viewing another person's experience, I spent most of my time alone. Tuning out the energy and vibrations of people came easy when I was alone or near water – somehow water deflected my hyper-sensitive psychic ability, so I sought calm hanging around the beach behind the recreation complex.

I began to feel weak when alone. The lightness of my body became heavy and my conscious mind hit me the hardest. I began viewing life through the eyes of my experience before my spiritual reprieve.

It was harsh returning to this worldly reality. I felt like I was falling into my body ever so slowly, and with each breath, I reached for my guides, as benevolent as they were. I walked the twelve kilometres, and before I realized, I had returned to Uranium City from Eldorado.

As I was walking around the road bend, I met a man on the road. I recognized him. He asked if he could join me. I liked his energy. He was kindhearted and a good soul, so I said yes.

It was a beautiful day. The sun was hot. I wanted to go swimming at the beach near town. Taking a shortcut on a bush trail leading to the lake, my spirit guides continued slowly bringing me back to consciousness. I feared not being able to sense them as intimately, though they remained with me.

Along the trail we talked. Paul introduced himself and said he'd noticed me for some time. He was happy to finally meet me. I blushed. Sensing his attraction toward me, I ignored it. I only wanted to be in his company to enjoy the day.

The trail was desolate. The only people that used it were a Dene family who lived in the bush off the highway where they still lived a traditional lifestyle on the land.

As we walked, we came upon a mattress on a hill. Paul smiled and said, "Thanks for bringing me here." I knew then he had the wrong idea. We stopped and Paul suggested we take a break and lie down. My spirit saddened. I didn't want to do anything and was hurt that he assumed this is why I asked him to join me.

I didn't say anything as we lay on the mattress. Paul took me in his arms. He tried to kiss me. Tears came to my eyes. My spirit broke. As I cried, clouds moved in on a gust of wind, hiding the sun. The universe cried with my spirit. Within seconds, the sky became grey and overcast as I wept.

Paul held me close when he saw that I was crying, trying to comfort me, "I'm sorry. I was hoping you wanted to... Don't cry. It's okay."

I cried as my guides ascended into the heavens. They left me in the arms of a kind man. I said good-bye to my angels as they gracefully returned my spirit to my conscious mind.

Paul held me until I resumed my body, empty and scared for my sanity. We lay a while before he walked me to town. He asked if I would be okay. I thanked him before leaving. Not knowing where I was going, I walked until I found a place to sleep.

FEARING HUMAN CONTACT

W hat memories I had of people caring became distorted. I couldn't and wouldn't allow myself to feel loved by anyone. Fearing human contact, I remained detached and unfeeling.

I came to the attention of the local RCMP and Social Services.

I was having coffee at the hotel when the RCMP picked me up, temporarily placing me in foster care before putting me on a plane back to Mom, who now lived in Fort Chipewyan. Social Services and my family had decided it was best to send me back to her. No one else was willing to take me in; their efforts in the past had been rudely resisted by me.

Mom appeared worn down and tired, and one night she flew into a fit of rage when my sisters were out late. She tried to hit me when I told her I didn't blame them. I grabbed her fist mid-air and swore to her that I would never allow her to hit me again.

After that night, she removed herself from me altogether and only seemed to tolerate me. Soon, I began feeling sick in the morning, so I went to the nursing station to see the doctor who flew in once a week. After he examined me, he informed me I was three months pregnant. The doctor then suggested some alternatives, including aborting the baby. Being pregnant at fourteen, in his opinion, was too young.

I left the nursing station with one thing in mind.

I didn't want to burden Mom with a baby, so I made arrangements to live with a former boyfriend in Saskatoon. It wasn't Wayne's child, which didn't matter to him: his concern was for me. Wayne was willing to help me get on my feet.

I left Mom and my sisters a month before my fifteenth birthday.

I arrived safely in Saskatoon and settled into a common-law relationship with Wayne. After my fifteenth birthday, I began hemorrhaging. I phoned a girlfriend and told her what was happening; she told me to go to the hospital immediately. I phoned a taxi and left. Wayne was at work, but I told his brother, Harold. He said for me to phone him once I knew what was going on and that he would let Wayne know once he got home.

The doctor had to operate to remove a cyst. So he said.

I lie on the table in pain, floating over my body. The doctor is disgusted and annoyed as he reaches for a scalpel. An obese nurse nods. He takes the scalpel and slices my flesh open a few centimetres beneath my belly button, haphazardly cutting my skin deeply to my panty line. A young nurse looks up at him with shock but seems afraid to say anything while the senior nurse coldly watches over. My skin is pulled apart and the doctor examines my womb. The young nurse appears shocked by his unprofessional malice. Within seconds he has removed a tiny foetus and my left ovary. The young nurse, appalled, looks to her senior nurse for understanding but is ignored. Both nurses are ordered to clean up. Blood is sponged and the ten-centimetre cut is closed with crude stitches.

My tiny unborn baby is carried away. I'm watching the doctor, floating above and feeling his anger and racism toward me, wondering why. I know he is justifying his actions. He doesn't think another Indian girl should bear children, and in his mind, he is doing society a favour. The young nurse leaves the operating room in tears; the senior nurse remains smug in support of the doctor's procedure.

After the operation, I lay in bed afraid, alone, and lonely. The hospital staff had contacted Mom for her authorization. I was underage. I missed Mom and wished someone were with me. My abdomen and uterus throbbed. I fell asleep.

The next day, Wayne came to see me at the hospital to ask me to move out once I was released. His former girlfriend was pregnant and she was moving in. I agreed. The only person I could think of contacting was a social worker I knew in Uranium City. Kathy had allowed me to stay with her for a few weeks when I lived there. I phoned her, explaining my circumstances as best I could, and asked if she could help.

Kathy agreed to bring me back to Uranium City to live with her until she could make other arrangements for me, and then she invited me to spend Christmas with her and her family. It was two months before Christmas. Wayne allowed me to stay at his house until Kathy could pick me up.

Kathy remained in touch with me, explaining she would be travelling to her hometown in southern Saskatchewan during the Christmas holiday break, one week before Christmas. By the time Kathy arrived in Saskatoon to pick me up, I wasn't talking or eating, and was barely able to function enough to do menial work around the house, or care for myself.

My body was numb and my mind void with the exception of making the next manoeuvre absolutely required of me. It seemed I slept until Kathy arrived. I packed my meagre belongings, said good-bye to Wayne and his girlfriend, feeling so deeply forlorn that their voices were barely audible.

In Kathy's vehicle, I remained detached and silent during the drive. When we arrived at her sister-in-law's house, her relatives welcomed us in holiday cheer, but I remained mute. I slept the first night; my parched throat reminded me to drink water.

For the following three days, I sat among strangers. I hadn't eaten; nibbling on Christmas dinner took effort. I went to bed after everyone left for a party, but unbeknownst to me, Kathy's sister-in-law Carina and her husband both stayed behind. He later staggered into my bedroom while I was sleeping, startling me as he towered over me while taking his pants off, telling me, "I know what you need."

I knew he was going to rape me, so I screamed for his wife, who was passed out upstairs. I didn't stop screaming until he left. Carina hadn't woken, but my screaming prevented the rape. Kathy returned soon after he left. I was sobbing in the bedroom. She heard me when she checked in on me, asking me what was wrong. I told her, explaining that I had scared the man away before he had a chance to do anything.

The next day she took me to a doctor to ensure that I was okay. I sat in the doctor's office after he examined me. His eyes became teary as he looked at me with sincere empathy. He asked what the incision on my abdomen was from, which he said was healing well. I said nothing.

He said that in his professional opinion there was no medical reason for any doctor to make incisions so haphazardly or bluntly. I still wouldn't respond. Both he and a nurse encouraged me to talk. They told me I had had a nervous breakdown. They pleaded with me to tell them what had happened. I looked at him.

It was such a simple question. "What happened?"

My mind spiralled into the crevices of my childhood. The sexual abuse, the hopelessness, rapes, drugs, alcohol, men, and homelessness. Vivid images of being butchered during the operation. I subconsciously held my breath as I thought about what the surgeon had said to me after the operation: "Your chance of becoming pregnant is less than that of an average woman."

I knew it hadn't been a dream.

These memories and images cascading in front of my eyes in merciless damnation, I whispered to the doctor and nurse, "I was born. That's what happened."

The doctor recommended antibiotics. I thought of Mom and the pills she took and said no. I asked if I could leave and raced out of the doctor's office before either the nurse or doctor agreed. As we drove back to Kathy's sister-in-law's, all the while remaining numb and distant, I told her the doctor said I had had a nervous breakdown.

In the following days I forced myself to eat and drink, until I revived enough strength to function.

We returned to Uranium City two days later.

Winter had retired and spring awoke. Time mended the trauma my body had endured since the operation. The ten-centimetre horizontal scar between my belly button and panty line left an ugly wound, a reminder of an event I couldn't erase, and something else I stored in my closet of skeletons mounting high.

Memories of my childhood faded into restless nightmares of being raped at thirteen. I had lost myself in a lifestyle where I repeatedly allowed statutory rape to occur amongst sexual preda-tors, resulting in a suicide attempt at fourteen, a psychotic col-lapse and a nervous breakdown at fifteen.

The dark days of my past subsided until the desire to live resumed.

I went back to work as a cook in a mining camp, earning good money throughout the spring and summer. Unwilling to move back with either of my parents, I meandered down a path of common-law relationships, living with men out of survival, much like collecting spare change. Accounts were opened for emergencies.

Moving from Uranium City to La Ronge, I shacked up with a pilot I had met in a camp. I lived with Carl for two months until he found out I was underage and asked me to move out. Then a girlfriend and I rented an apartment, which lasted one month. I decided to leave town when the authorities were on my trail again. If I remained in La Ronge, I would have been apprehended by Social Services. I was fifteen, going to bars and not having much luck with keeping a job.

I returned to Uranium City and went back to work, once again living with Dad and his common-law wife.

A CELESTIAL STAR CHILD

While I was running away, my cousin Latasha remained on the fringes of my life, but she had been my childhood best friend. I was ten years old when Mom tried – once again unsuccessfully – to leave Jake. That time, we ended up with Latasha's mom, Aunt Margo, in Fort McMurray. Latasha and I started hanging out, and we got along in spite of our strong personalities. Later, I'd often end up at their doorstep, needing a place to live. Aunt Margo always allowed me to stay with them; she understood my circumstances and never turned me away.

Latasha and I talked about everything, and shared some secrets, though I never told her what Jake did to me. Latasha was skinny, with long, beautiful legs, wavy, light brown hair, sensuous, full lips and round, butterfly hazel eyes – serious eyes, with an edge of wit and humour. I liked her wacky sense of humour. She was beautiful, and I didn't mind standing in her shadow. I didn't want the attention – I was too self-conscious to enjoy it. Attention made me paranoid, and it was easy to go unnoticed in her company – she had a way of being the centre of everyone's attention.

Latasha came back into my life when she moved to Uranium City to live briefly with my Dad and his common-law wife. I lived with them too. We partied hard, enjoying our youth. Unbeknownst to Latasha, she was my barometer of what was typical behaviour for a teenager. She was vivacious, a popular new girl in town; everyone liked her light-hearted attitude. She didn't act out with "wild child" antics, and she grounded me when I got carried away. And despite the gossip about me, she remained loyal to our friendship. I was redeemed in Dad's eyes for hanging out with her.

My fifteenth year came and went, with all its heartache and recovery. My sixteenth year was spent with Latasha, as we enjoyed our adolescent renaissance in Fort McMurray and Uranium City, where I met Dan.

The first day I saw Dan standing at the restaurant counter paying his bill, I was instantly attracted to his bright blue eyes and dark blond hair. He looked rugged, hot, and when he walked out of the restaurant, I admired the way he filled out his jeans. We eventually met one night in the bar lounge. I was drunk, looking for guys to invite to a party at my sister Sara's. Dan didn't know it then, but I was only sixteen. He was twenty-one.

It wasn't until after we started dating that it occurred to me that I should confess my age. Dan took me out for dinner, ordered wine, and as we ate dinner, I sat mortified, waiting for the waitress to ask for my identification. She didn't. I knew then that Dan assumed I was of legal age. At that point, I decided that if I told him, he likely wouldn't want to see me, so I said nothing.

Latasha moved in with her boyfriend, but we remained close, hanging out throughout the summer. Latasha and I continued partying as Dan and I got to know each other – dating, going for walks, to dances and out for coffee. Dan was fun and sentimental, and though he tried, we never ventured beyond holding hands and kissing. He was working in Uranium City for the summer in construction, as a framer.

Dan was born and raised in a small prairie town. His father was a teacher, and his mom a homemaker and physiotherapist. Dan was the second eldest of four children. His parents adopted another son and daughter, both Native. His adopted brother, Daryl, was physically handicapped and remained at home with his parents. Sadly, his adopted sister moved out as soon as she could, in search of her biological family.

He adored his parents and siblings, and that moved me more than anything. When he talked about his family, his stories were light-hearted and funny, spoken through his boisterous and hearty laughter. I'd listen to him reminisce, envious and happy for him. I, on the other hand, had few stories to share of happy times with my family, so I bragged about my sisters and offered few details of my mom, and that I lived at home with Dad, as if it were a content situation instead of an intrusion as far as his common-law wife was concerned.

After a few weeks of dating, I was taken by surprise when he invited me to southern Saskatchewan to meet his family. I accepted, and when we returned to Uranium City, we moved in with my dad. Dan continued working in construction for the remainder of the summer. When they were finished their contract and it was time for Dan to leave, we left together. I couldn't have been happier.

We stayed with his family before moving to the west coast, where Dan had been accepted at Simon Fraser University.

I was taken aback with how healthy and normal Dan's family seemed compared to mine. I was bewildered to the point that I asked Dan, in all sincerity, if his dad ever slapped his mom around. Dan was shocked, and then when he realized that I was serious, he informed me that he had never witnessed his father raise a hand to his mother. I couldn't wrap my mind around the concept of not witnessing or being subjected to violence.

Sitting down for meals with his family became one of the most nerve-wracking times of day for me. I didn't know how to behave. I was fearful of appearing a slob; I cut every slice of food on my plate gingerly. Mindful of mixing my food rather than eating everything separately, I picked at morsels of my meal, chewing with my mouth closed. The effort that went into the ritual of eating properly often left me with no appetite.

It wasn't that Dan's family was prudish; they were common folk who lived humbly, yet I'd never experienced the simplicity of family life. I felt like I was living in an episode of "Happy Days," a female Fonzie married to Richie Cunningham, inept and ill-equipped to perform the most mundane tasks, such as how to conduct oneself at the dinner table.

I managed to apply my work skills in the kitchen, cleaning and sometimes cooking, staying busy so I didn't have to pretend I was comfortable when I wasn't. Regardless of Dan's family's efforts to make me feel at home, in the beginning, I was a wreck trying to hide my anxiety of fitting in.

His parents didn't drink daily; in fact, his dad didn't drink at all. There was no one beating on anyone, unless I started a pillow fight or playfully wrestled with his adopted brother. The family sat down together in the evening, filling the cushioned couch with fully relaxed bodies; some consumed the easy chair, while others lay on the pillows on the floor. We watched television, visited, and conversed with each other.

There were family picnics at their cottage, and everyone's birthday was celebrated with a family gathering. Dan's parents' home was constantly filled with his siblings coming and going. When it was time to go to bed, everyone said goodnight, and I lay awake, in awe of what was the most wholesome and loving environment I'd ever known.

With no one drinking, I had no option but to refrain from functioning the only way I knew how: drunk. My compulsion and desire to drink was restrained, unless Dan and I went out, and then I let my hair down and proceeded to get blitzed and make an ass of myself. At the end of most of the evenings we went out, I was back to my staggering, belligerent, rowdy self, much to Dan's discomfort. My swearing and sarcastic street language and defensive attitude entertained some people and offended others. Going out with Dan's friends wasn't something he enjoyed as much I did in the end.

In spite of myself, I was painfully ill at ease with Dan's family, in an atmosphere so different from what I'd known, or lived, I might as well have been in Germany or Taiwan. In time, their acceptance and love nurtured my tortured mind as I slowly thrived at their hearth. My mother-in-law charmed me with her candid character, while my father-in-law tickled me with his fun, wily personality. The rough edges of my tough persona and carefree attitude smoothed enough to resemble someone even I didn't know: me. Privately, I lived with a horrifying fear that someone would realize the blatantly obvious: I didn't belong, and I was a fake. Paranoid of being found out, I pretended I wasn't the least bit fazed by the normality of daily life, in a home that wasn't accompanied with that familiar feeling that came with an all-out shit-kicking, knock-your-teeth-out, fists-flying, immobilizing fear and neglect I was used to.

I posed as a well-mannered young lady who comprehended the rationale of ensuring we had all the fixings for supper. Hell, I was grateful to be eating without being stabbed by a fork for lifting someone else's food off their plate. I was wound up tighter than a Tasmanian devil, ready to jump out of my skin most days, running late for rehearsals in a play I hadn't studied my lines for. Every day felt like an act, and I was too mesmerized with the set to concentrate on my part. I ad libbed, all the while confused and freaked out.

When I didn't feel safe, I cuddled Dan for security, rolled up on his lap until I felt calm enough to remove myself from his arms. There was a lot of cuddling.

Life with Mom and my sisters remained locked away in a suitcase I buried. I knew what they were going through, and I felt guilty for having Dan in my life.

My safety and oasis with Dan was something I had only dreamt about. It didn't seem fair that I should have it so good. In spite of my insecurities, I missed Mom and my sisters, and the chaotic comfort that came with the insanity of life on the edge. It was what I related to, all I had known or experienced.

My mixed emotions caused me more anxiety. I didn't know where to draw the line of loyalty between my sisters and Dan. Everything was blurred. I felt bound to the ties of my past and the pain I shared with my sisters. I had managed to claw my way out of the hole in the drywall, while my sisters remained in the darkness. Standing in the light beside Dan, I wanted to crawl back into the hole and rescue them.

In the midst of all these changes, I was sober and clean longer then I'd been for any length of time since I was thirteen. As a result, I now had to experience my feelings. I felt everything, and all that I had run from in my childhood came back, haunting me as I tried to conceal my secrets, secrets I couldn't talk about, secrets that made me feel like a lost child. Then I'd crawl into Dan's arms, on his lap, and breathe, just breathe in his love until the terror subsided.

I craved him and the security of his touch. Dan just thought I was affectionate, and he never denied his love. My new family engulfed me with unconditional love, and despite some talk from a few of the locals who referred to Dan's family as "Indian lovers," I was welcomed as part of their clan.

We stayed with Dan's family for the remainder of the summer before moving to the west coast. We became engaged in Surrey, British Columbia, while living with my Aunt Grace and Uncle Hank, Dad's younger brother. They were kind enough to allow us to live in a trailer parked on their lot until we rented our own place. We found a small two-bedroom house, which we shared with a huge rat that lived beneath the sink; it came out in the middle of the night for leftovers, until I learned to throw out the garbage before going to bed.

On my seventeenth birthday, I told Dan how old I was. By then, it was of no consequence. Dan admitted that had he known, he likely wouldn't have pursued the relationship.

I soon found work at the Simon Fraser University campus café, as a cook. Shortly after I started working there, the smell of food, coffee and every other aroma made me nauseous. I went to the doctor and found out it was morning sickness. I was three months pregnant.

Wanting a healthy pregnancy, I didn't drink and I quit smoking. I now had no means of escaping the nightmares of being sexually abused, which surfaced with a force so intense, I thought I was losing my mind. Yet I couldn't talk to Dan about what was happening to me.

Some nights were unbearable. Dan often woke to find me crying hysterically. When he tried to console me, I'd scream as his face turned into the face of someone who was trying to molest me, someone I'd have to fight off, push away, until Dan was forced to wrestle me until I calmed down or woke up. Then I'd fall asleep in his arms again. By morning, in spite of Dan's obvious concern, I wouldn't talk about the night before. The memories that surfaced had a life of their own, and I had no control.

Once we got over the surprise of my pregnancy, we decided to move back to the prairies. With a baby on the way, Dan put his education on the back burner. I quit my job, as we prepared to move back to Saskatchewan. I was happy we were moving, to be near Dan's family and closer to mine. In Saskatoon we settled into a one-bedroom apartment. Dan went back to work in construction, earning enough money for us to survive, and I started attending church in my quest to stay sane.

I became rigid and paranoid rather than sane, swinging to extremes of cult religious phantasm. I had confided in the pastor and his wife my nightmares, not mentioning my sexual abuse. They convinced me that I was possessed, and then they arranged to perform an exorcism on me. The only spirit they evoked was that of an enraged, violent child who swore and screamed as they prayed over me, laying their hands on my body in an effort to denounce the demons. After the exorcism, I stepped back from my involvement with the church and resumed living my life as peacefully as I could. Not that I felt relieved as a result of this bizarre exorcism – I felt the need to nest.

I loved being pregnant, feeling this child move inside me; Dan and I were certain it was a boy for all the kicking and athletic manoeuvring in my womb. I cosily slipped on a Suzy Homemaker apron and discovered I was good at it. I loved baking. I wouldn't buy bread; I baked our own. I remembered how Grandma Isabelle and Mom could easily cook a meal, seemingly out of nothing. The recipe was easy to follow: make the most of what you have.

I'd wait for Dan to return home, anxious to smell the scent of wood on him, from a hard day of carpentry and sweat, waiting to hold him, and for him to hold me, and caress my huge belly. Once he got home from work, I beamed over a hot meal, satisfied with myself. Dan devoured his meat and potatoes, then we'd relax and talk, mostly about the day or the baby.

I gained weight fast, and the baby grew faster. I talked aloud to the baby, reading books and conversing. If I was emotional before being pregnant, my pregnancy turned me into a weeping willow, with the sentimentality of an innocent child. I cried over anything. Tired, I slept peacefully.

Feeling this tiny human being grow inside me, I patiently waited, day by day, counting every blessing I had in my life. After his family got over Dan not completing his education, they accepted it and waited anxiously with us too, for our new addition to the clan.

The baby was the first grandchild in my family, and my sisters and Mom were happy for us. Dad and his common-law wife were excited as well. It seemed our baby mended most of our wounds, as much as they could be mended. Everyone was anxious and excited for us, and at seventeen, engaged and pregnant, blissful and healthy, I lived out a fantasy come true: to have a family and be happy. I had a handsome, caring and considerate man who loved and adored me, when I wasn't driving him crazy with my emotionalism. Together, we had what we needed, as we prepared for our family to grow. I remained grounded in my daily routine and stayed in touch with my sisters and Mom long distance.

I developed close friendships with Dan's sister Katlin and his mom. They both visited often, and Dan's mom always provided us with a care package of food, whether we needed it or not; she simply wanted to share, and it was a welcome offering of affection. I hand-sewed stuffed animals. My Aunt Grace in British Columbia made a baby quilt for us. When we had extra money, I'd shop for things we would need once the baby was born.

My world revolved around this child yet to be born.

It seemed nothing would, or could, penetrate my happiness, until one day, Jake came back to remind me of everything I'd left behind. I was five months pregnant when I received word that Jake was dead. I went home to Fort Chipewyan for the funeral.

It was confusing to grieve for the man who had terrorized us. Jake was part of our childhood, and we had all bonded with him, as children do with adults in spite of the pain and fear they inflict. I felt ashamed and guilty because I was relieved Jake couldn't hurt us anymore, yet sad that he'd met his death under tragic circumstances.

Four months after Jake's funeral, Matthew was born. I was eighteen. The first moment I held Matthew in my arms, his tiny fingers reached out to me. We looked into each other's eyes as if to say, "What took you so long?" Life had new meaning, and the point of living lay in my arms needing to be nurtured and fed.

Dan and I arranged for my two youngest sisters, Ruth and Tania, to live with us for a year. I was very rigid with them. Dan tolerated my notions of religious purity, unless he was defending my sisters, who were usually under house arrest because they didn't behave as saintly as I thought they should. I imposed a religious regime that was almost cult-like on my sisters. I brought them to church every Sunday, and we prayed every day; I made them throw out records, at least the ones I thought had subliminal satanic chants when played backwards. I ruled my household in the name of God, yet despite my overbearing presence, my sisters adored Matthew and did well in school, and sometimes our home life resembled normality. I was always striving for normality.

We got married, against the better judgement of a pastor we sought counsel from. In his opinion, Dan and I were incompatible. We didn't take heed of his premonition, but the likelihood of a pastor blessing the marriage of a woman he had performed an exorcism on was slim.

OLD HABITS

My sisters finished the school year and I brought them back to Fort Chipewyan, where I found comfort in the familiarity of the community. Dormant habits returned overnight, and I reverted back to drinking, smoking and partying.

My compulsion to drink didn't sneak up on me – it lassoed me with an alcoholic euphoria, and the craving held me prisoner. Being home among familiar people, places, and surroundings, I disregarded what I had left behind with my husband. It started innocently enough: one drink led to another, and on and on, and before I knew what day it was, I had drunk enough to make up for lost time.

I partied the whole time I was home.

My sisters chose to remain with Mom in Fort Chipewyan rather than return to Saskatoon with me, where my drinking progressed rapidly and I picked up my old vice of acid and cocaine while my husband worked out of town. Partying became more of a priority than parenting, and our marriage fell apart.

When Dan returned from the Northwest Territories, I went to work at a mine in northern Saskatchewan. Matthew was nineteen months old. Within two months, I had left my husband and abandoned Matthew with him. Relapsing into a lifestyle of one-night stands and carousing, I moved back to Fort McMurray.

Reformed puritan was transformed into biker bitch. The lifestyle suited me; I wore my black leather jacket with attitude. It was my armour of not caring about anything or anyone, especially when it came to numbing the pain of abandoning Matthew.

Passing out at parties and drinking till I puked were fine with the people I drank with. Everyone did it. I wasn't good at expressing my feelings, and talking drunken talk usually led to sobbing into my beer about how much I missed my kid.

In Fort McMurray, I worked as a bar server, which allowed me to drink all the time. Despite my efforts to forget about my marriage and my son, I couldn't reconcile being away from Matthew, so I made arrangements with Dan to send Matthew to me. I ended up neglecting him, and often dropped him off with friends and family when I was going out, which was most of the time. Dan eventually had to drive to Fort McMurray to get Matthew. This sobered me up long enough that I decided to try and make amends with Dan and save our marriage. Dan was willing to try, providing I sought help for my drinking, so I went into rehab after I moved back to Saskatchewan.

I was nineteen the first time I went into treatment, but my efforts to remain sober were futile. I didn't appreciate the value of stability or raising a family. Choosing to live according to my inclinations, I left Matthew with Dan and returned to Alberta, where I made my routes between Fort Chipewyan and Fort McMurray, bootlegging.

I continued to travel back and forth between Saskatoon and Fort McMurray, raising Matthew in brief intervals of sobriety in Saskatoon, where I sobered up for three to six months at a time.

During a stint of sobriety in 1985, I attended the centennial of the Riel Resistance at Batoche. I spent most of my time visiting my girlfriend Rosanne while taking in the festivities. There were jigging contests, fiddling, and square dancing, and the grounds were filled with campers and tents around the arbour, where the main events took place. Homage was paid to those who died during the Riel Resistance at a pilgrimage to the graves, where a pipe ceremony and Catholic prayer service was held. Rosanne gathered wildflowers to place on her grandmother's grave. I sat near a grave, and then Rosanne sat beside me. Maria situated herself near the pipe ceremony by Gabrial Dumont's grave.

Ironically, an large wooden cross towered over us, casting a shadow onto us across a barbed wire fence. The priest stood opposite the cross, outside the graveyard, and the pipe ceremony took place on our side of the fence, opposite the cross. Two ancient methods of prayer and ceremony commenced as the priest began to pray at the same time as the pipe was lit. Most people were seated in the graveyard, at the pipe ceremony.

I came to understand and appreciate the significance of oral history and knowledge. I listened to Maria and several storytellers bring the Riel Resistance to life in stories passed on through time. Each storyteller spoke of an event that changed Métis history. I knew this history would never be interpreted honestly in Canadian terms of reference or standard historical documentation. The keepers of our true history, Indian or Métis, would remain within the spirit of our people, to be passed on through the storytellers.

They spoke of the men who had fought and died for Métis rights. I tried to imagine what the women had endured, with their children, for their children. They were forced to survive as "Road Allowance" people, whose place in this country was denied. Though land and money scrip was offered as a result of the Riel Resistance, scrip wasn't always honoured.

The stories of their lives became an extension of mine, and ever so gently, the grandmothers validated my life, enough for me to appreciate my Métis ancestry and history. In the middle of the night, in Maria's cabin at Batoche, Rosanne and I shared our stories too. A dimly lit candle, pot of hot tea, shared between two women reminiscing about times gone by and hopeful of times yet to come. We laughed and cried, as soul sisters do, and late into the night we weaved our history by the warmth of a wood-burning stove, expressing ourselves honestly, strengthening one another in the process.

Outside the cabin, the river flowed; the wind whispered a song of a prairie grass dance as the spirits of our ancestors laid themselves to rest on the land. At the campground, late into the night, lovers crooned to fiddlers' tunes, as a fury of feet clicked to the Red River jig inside the main arbour. Fires crackled alongside several camps. Laughter and voices filled the void of night.

During the gathering, I was introduced to Dwayne. He instantly reminded me of Grandpa Jonas. The depths of his dark brown owl eyes were hypnotizing. A gifted storyteller and entertainer, his voice captured his audience. It seemed the spirit of his stories pulled you in, and took you wherever he wanted to take you.

Dwayne and I instantly formed a kinship. We visited long enough to know we wanted to spend more time together. Dwayne was busy and so was I, but we agreed to remain in touch.

In Saskatoon, I returned to school to upgrade myself, but my drinking soon interfered. I returned to work in a bar. Serving booze conveniently subsidized my drinking. I went into treatment two more times as I continued going back and forth to my husband – as often as he would take me back – until I became pregnant with another man's child. It was a fallopian pregnancy and the foetus ruptured my fallopian tube.

On the night I went to the hospital, Dan didn't believe anything was wrong with me. We were having a screaming argument when the rupture occurred. I bent over, faint and unable to stand. I told Dan I needed to get to emergency. At first he refused to take me, suggesting I was having a mental breakdown. I knew something was terribly wrong and phoned a taxi, but Dan then agreed to drive me.

While I lay in and out of consciousness in the City Hospital Emergency Department, he told a nurse on nightshift that I was seeking sympathy and attention. My bladder felt like it was going to explode, so I told the nurse I needed to use the washroom, but I almost passed out while attempting to stand. The nurse on duty immediately contacted a doctor, who arrived within minutes. I had an ultrasound and was rushed to the operating room.

I lost two litres of blood internally and was clinically dead, then revived. The doctor saved my life, and I lost my baby.

I knew I was going to die before the operation and said a simple prayer: "God, I need to be here to watch my son become a man."

After the operation, I woke to Dan holding my hand. He was crying, asking for my forgiveness. All I could think about was how I had wronged him.

Once I regained consciousness, being in the hospital triggered memories of when I was fifteen. I regressed into a familiar place of despair and hopelessness. Yet something changed in me after the operation. I had died, if only momentarily, yet there was more to it. Whatever it was, I knew my life no longer involved being married to Dan.

When I recovered, I moved back to Alberta, abandoning my son once more with Dan.

Dan allowed me to have access to Matthew until he became aware of how much my drinking had progressed, and then he gave me an ultimatum: either sober up or lose Matthew. I kept drinking.

I moved to Edmonton. Matthew was living with me. He was three. I made yet another attempt to sober up and get a life. Uncle Fred had died several years before, and Aunt May frequently stayed with me as she too continued moving throughout western Canada, going back and forth between Saskatoon, Edmonton, and Vancouver. She'd cared for Matthew when he was two and three, during her stays with me in Saskatoon and Edmonton.

Chery and Dwayne lived in the same building as me. They rented a suite in the basement of an older character building on 110 Street off Jasper Avenue. I lived on the third floor. Chery often babysat Matthew for me. She adored him – most people did. Matthew was cute, with an old man spirit, wise beyond his childhood years.

Dwayne and I visited often, as neighbours, and we came to know each other deeply. I would sit and listen to him tell stories for hours. He spoke of his passions in life: the land, his children, his crafts, writing, politics, and his personal history as a foster child. He and Chery had gone through the system together, and their stories were not much different from other Native children in care. I hadn't disclosed to him, or anyone, the details of my childhood. I kept my secrets, but he knew. Dwayne looked into my soul, and he knew.

While Dwayne occupied himself with making crafts, red willow baskets, birchbark baskets, working with hide and beads, Chery was a clothing designer, and both artists had mastered their crafts. Dwayne had a collection of poetry and writings. He was a political activist, and he enjoyed working with youth as a junior warden officer. The summer we met at the centennial of the Riel Resistance, he had canoed from Edmonton to Batoche with a brigade of Junior Forest youth.

In the company of Dwayne and Chery, I found comfort and solace as we shared bannock and soup, cigarettes and coffee, joking around and telling stories. Dwayne had an old man spirit too – he was of the land, and in the city he appeared out of his element, yet he remained in Edmonton to continue with his activism. We were drawn to each other for many reasons, and our stories unified us, stories that ratified our existence in an otherwise cold and foreign system we felt lost in.

In their apartment, the smell of smoked hide, sweetgrass, fungus, and sage hung in the air, fragrances that reminded me of the bush. Dwayne's scent was of a bush man: smoky-musky earth grounded into muskeg-peppermint-tea-leaves, stirring my spirit. He had good medicine in his blood: it cleansed me, and his love nurtured my heart.

He invited me over for coffee on many occasions. Most times we just needed to be in each other's company. Dwayne was a ladies man and adored by many women, yet he reserved a special place for us. I knew I would lose myself in him if I ventured further than we allowed ourselves to wander when alone. Dwayne's dark brown eyes were a valley I dared tread, easily losing my balance when I gazed too long. His full lips and strong features stole me every time, and he knew it. Yet my affection for Dwayne wasn't lustful. He was more than an attractive man to me: he was a brother, and he respected me as his sister. Though we tempted each other teasingly, we loved from a distance. He just needed to walk with me for a while, and I with him, two tired souls who took comfort in finding a lost friend, far off the bush trail.

Dwayne and Chery came into my life as I attempted to make the transition into Edmonton, a city that held memories I had spent most of my life running from, where the streets I was raised on still held me captive, chaining me emotionally, pulling me into the sewers of my worst nightmares, nightmares I had no strength left to fight. Dwayne and Chery gave me hope through our stories and laughter.

I continued chasing the elusive dream of finding myself, and went back to Fort Chip. Matthew returned to Dan, and I went on a drunk that lasted several months. I left Fort Chip, or rather was escorted out of town after a drunk, and landed in Fort

McMurray, where I decided to take a "lazy man's holiday" and hitchhiked with a girlfriend, Anita, back and forth between Fort McMurray, Edmonton, and Saskatoon.

After Anita and I returned to Fort McMurray, she remained there, and I carried on down the whiskey highway. Returning to Edmonton, I remained a daily drinker and drug addict. Once again, I begged Dan to take me back. I was on my way to Saskatchewan when he agreed to try again. I had no money and couldn't bring myself to ask for his help, so I went out and hustled an old man at the Cecil Hotel, only to find myself chasing a fix.

I ended up working the streets, trying to stay sober long enough to save money to buy a bus ticket to Saskatchewan. My cravings for cocaine and alcohol kept me on the streets, where I lived with another girl who was also working. I couldn't stay sober long enough to keep any of the money I made, and I kept telling myself, tomorrow I'll stop. But the streets and the lifestyle swallowed me, and I couldn't exit.

I had given up when Dwayne saw me standing on 94 Street and 104 Avenue. He walked up to me and asked in bewilderment, "Are you working?" I couldn't look Dwayne in the eye, so I didn't say anything. He quietly said, "You don't belong here...," then walked away.

Dwayne's words whiplashed, and the impact woke me, reminding me of when Matthew was two and half years old and he asked, "Mommy where are you going?"

I was in a rush, getting ready to go to the bar. "I'm going to the store to buy bread."

Matthew knew I was lying. He started to cry, "Mommy don't drink beer, it's no good for you."

I couldn't run out the door fast enough as I witnessed myself through my son.

"Mommy, don't go!"

I shut the door and left Matthew crying for me to come back. I had done onto my son what had been done unto me. Matthew stood behind the closed door crying, begging me not to leave him.

Soon after this had happened, my dad called Dan and asked him to drive to Fort McMurray to get Matthew. I'd neglected him and dropped him off with family and friends too often.

During the year that followed before the day Dwayne saw me on the street, I rarely saw Matthew.

THE TENDER YEARS

I gave up on myself, and I doubt I would have tried one last time if Dwayne hadn't found me standing on the corner that day, reminding me of the one reason I had to live, Matthew. I couldn't put Matthew through what I'd gone through. The day after I saw Dwayne, on June 28, 1986, I had my last drink.

"You don't belong here..." The pain and disappointment in Dwayne's eyes sobered me up. Someone cared, if only I would too. I was twenty-two years old.

I stayed messed up and confused for a long time after I sobered up, not knowing how to cope with my emotions or life in general. The pain and angst I had internalized from my child-hood remained a current beneath calm waters.

Coming in off the streets was hard. I had to leave behind everything I knew about myself. Losing my tough, street-savvy attitude, along with my biker bitch persona, was like letting go of an old friend. I reacted like a mad dog on a short leash, tied to the streets as I whimpered alone in my pain, snarling at strangers passing by.

I had hundreds of days where I relapsed into old behaviours or attitudes. Sainthood isn't a prerequisite of sobriety, and I wasn't hung up on trying to be someone else. I didn't trust anyone. I remained paranoid and, for the most part, unfeeling and withdrawn. I didn't like feeling vulnerable, so when I started to, I shut down emotionally. With one exception: Matthew. With him, life's meaning remained the same as the first moment I had held him in my arms. Nothing else mattered, regardless of what was going on within me or around me; I mellowed with him near.

Dan and I agreed to share custody after our divorce: one school year with each parent. Matthew became my touchstone in life. Every time I saw him, he'd raise his arms as he ran toward me, and then we'd wrap ourselves around each other and hug for a long time. Matthew came back to live with me when he was five, and there were no more tears from him watching me drink beer, which also meant I could participate in his play, as a parent.

I naturally gravitated to the old neighbourhood in Edmonton, where I rented a two-bedroom house on 95 Street and 109 Avenue. I created a routine of waking with Matthew, cooking porridge and toast, and staying busy throughout the day, playing, visiting and being a mom, until supper settled both of us in quiet time, which was a welcome change from hangovers and loneliness.

By fall, life was going good, as far as I could tell. I was working, I had a truck, I was staying sober, and, to the best of my ability, I was caring for Matthew. After work one afternoon, though, I picked Matthew up from daycare and he asked shyly if he could live with his dad.

I didn't know where I'd gone wrong. In my mind, I was doing everything right, but Matthew was only five, and he missed his dad. I knew Matthew was used to visiting me for a weekend or a couple weeks at a time, and then he knew he would be returning to his dad. Apparently, he had decided it was time to go back. I could never keep Matthew from his dad because Dan was a loving, responsible father, and I cherished how close they were. I also understood Matthew's need for stability – he'd spent most of young life with Dan and Dan's family.

I swallowed my pride, phoned Dan, and told him Matthew wanted to live with him again. Dan was only too happy to have Matthew back. In order to earn Matthew's trust, I had to allow him to trust his own decisions. As young as he was, he knew what was best for him, and although I felt like a failure, I had to be unselfish and let go with love.

The day before I brought Matthew to Provost, Alberta, where Dan was teaching, I drove him into the country and parked on a hill overlooking miles of rolling hills. From where I parked, watching the sunset, my heart felt like it was sinking into the sky too. With loving clarity, the sunset inspired me. I said to my little man as I cuddled him close, "Every day the sun rises, and every night the sun sets, and just as sure as the sun will rise tomorrow, I will always love you, and when the sun sets, I will be holding you near my heart. No matter what, I'll be here for you." I placed my hand on his heart, and held him closer, folded in my arms, and then I wept.

My little man held me tighter as we cried. I wanted to take his pain away, but all I could do was cradle him back and forth as I hummed his song to him, comforting him as best I could. I knew how confusing and painful it was to be torn between two parents who lived apart, missing one when away with the other. The glimmering sun faded into the horizon as Matthew fell asleep in my arms.

After I left Matthew with Dan the next day, I drove away weak. My son humbled me when I realized what little I had to offer him, knowing how often I had neglected and abandoned him. He had the right to do what was in his own best interest. I understood he needed his dad, who had been there when I wasn't.

Making miles down the highway to visit Matthew every other weekend became my favourite road trip, or picking him up on holidays. Each time I picked Matthew up, I was sober. Over time, he was more and more at ease, knowing I wouldn't leave him with other people while he was with me, and as our visits increased, so did his trust in me and my behaviour.

In between visits with Matthew, I remained in contact with Dwayne and Chery. She eventually convinced me to model for her, and on a trip to Saskatoon, we did a fashion show at a fancy downtown hotel, and I also had a small part in a video on Native designers. I caught the acting bug and enjoyed modelling. My self-esteem was shot, but modelling helped me gain a sense of myself and my appearance that I'd never had before. Regardless of how unattractive I saw myself as, I walked the ramp with confidence; my spunk carried me, with sheer cockiness masquerading as grace.

I then had to make a choice: model and work part time as a consultant and live on the edge, or keep my position as a Native liaison counsellor, which provided stability. My free-spirited nature dictated to me like the wind, so I resigned from my position and immersed myself in work as a consultant.

IN THE MIRROR

As Matthew grew, I basked in his every discovery of the world around him, praising him in all his efforts, mindful not to criticize him, wanting desperately to be positive so as not to hurt his spirit with ridicule. I was so afraid of failing and, worse yet, of demeaning his inquisitive and curious mind.

There weren't enough hours in a day to hold him, hug him and listen to him. Dan and I spared no affection toward him. Dan had often held him as a baby, on his chest, while Matthew slept in the warmth of his father's pride. I wanted Matthew to feel loved, cared for and safe. I wanted him to have what I hadn't had with my parents.

Mom and I had never been close, but I still needed her to share the simple things – cooking, talking, sharing, shopping, hanging out, visiting – but the only pastime she offered was to drink with her. I no longer drank, so that shut the door altogether.

I hadn't seen her in some time, and wasn't even sure whether she lived in Fort Chip or Fort McMurray. Her whereabouts was solved one night when she arrived at my door, drunk, late in the evening. Though I was happy to see her, seeing her drunk triggered deep feelings in me, and I didn't know how to react. I went from an adult to a child within seconds.

She needed a place to stay. At first I was uncomfortable, and then I reluctantly offered my couch. While she made herself comfortable, I attempted to talk with her about myself and what I'd been doing with my life, only to realize what little common ground we shared. I settled for reciting a poem I had written for her. She cried and then passed out. I went to sleep feeling that familiar knot in my stomach and remained restless throughout the night. After thinking about it, I grew resentful at her for arriving at my doorstep unannounced, and the more I thought about it, the angrier I became at her intrusion into the sanctuary I had tried to create in my humble apartment.

It was apparent she needed a place to crash, which was okay: I had offered my home to friends who needed a place to sleep; why should it be any different with her? But it was. I didn't know why it was different, other than that she was drunk and hadn't even contacted me for several months. She just showed up, and I felt, once again, like I was being forced to care for her in her stupor.

The next day she left, and late at night, she phoned me from the York Hotel, drunk. She wanted to come over. The déjà vu was more than I could handle, and I said no. She laid on a thick serving of guilt. I cried myself to sleep like a baby. The guilt trip had its effect: I walked around an emotional wreck for the next few days, wondering whether she was okay.

When she did phone again, I explained to her – all the while shaking with raw nerves – that as a child, I had had no choice, but as an adult, I had choices, and I wasn't comfortable being around her when she drank. She said, "That's true," and we left it at that.

Unwilling to be responsible for my mom and siblings, I pulled in the welcome mat from everyone. I was only beginning to gain a sense of sanity in sobriety, and I knew I didn't have the energy to care for anyone other than Matthew and myself, and even that was more than enough at times.

Despite my need to let go, I didn't expect my sisters or Mom to understand. Instead, I was viewed as abandoning the family, as being selfish and inconsiderate of their needs. I, on the other hand, was determined to live my life.

My new job as a consultant was to facilitate workshops in remote communities on family violence, sexual abuse, alcoholism, and community development. As a team, we worked with groups of Aboriginal youth, varying in numbers of twenty to fifty at times. I wasn't trained, nor was I educated to work with youth in this capacity. All I had was my story. I was passionate and charismatic when talking, but I was not qualified for this intense work.

I believed in the mandate and concept until I realized the magnitude of the work, and after the fourth community, I decided I didn't agree with the methods. In two- to four-day periods, we tore open wounds, revealing extremely serious issues, and then left the communities incapacitated with pain. Often, these isolated communities had few if any resources to facilitate the necessary ongoing healing or follow-up on issues as serious as the disclosure of sexual abuse and family violence. I felt like a hypocrite. I hadn't faced my own sexual abuse issues, or any of the issues from my childhood.

When we travelled to Anchorage, Alaska, I knew without a doubt that I couldn't continue with this work. I was the guest speaker at a maximum-security penitentiary, where fifty hard-core prisoners attended my presentation. Lifers, rapists, and convicted murders were in the audience, but I wasn't the least bit intimidated. Three young women who were also prisoners were allowed to attend, which was exceptional under the circumstances.

I spoke for more than an hour. I took notice of one of the young women in the audience. She was crying, obviously unable to contain her grief. When I finished speaking, I wrote down my address and gave it to her and asked her to write me a letter.

On the last night of the conference, there was a round dance and feast. The drum beat consoled my restlessness and inner turmoil, calming me after hearing several stories of sexual abuse and ongoing trauma among so many young people. I admired the humanity of each individual who cried through their anguish. I tried to remain composed while images of my own childhood raged to the forefront of my consciousness. My maternal instincts desperately made me want to reach out to each child, to hold them, and all I could do was pray for blessings for every child as they bared their souls. Their truth liberated me from my own denial and gave me the courage to begin to face my past honestly.

I felt the Great Mystery carry me through a valley of souls in need of hope, and found hope myself. They were all so brave and unselfish, these children who came from a legacy of abuse. I considered how many youths I had met as a consultant and multiplied that number by the number of communities we *hadn't* been to. I realized that my childhood wasn't unique. This awareness hit me with an emotional tidal wave so intense that I was jarred beyond my self-loathing and self-pity and I became willing to begin my own personal healing journey.

Back in Edmonton, I felt compelled to visit my old neighbourhood. I drove past the house of horrors at 107 Avenue and 95 Street. It remained as abandoned and desolate as the memories that still made me anxious and sick with shame.

Many of the old buildings still stood: The gas station, where I conned money from an attendant who knew I was conning her, yet she ignored my lies. She probably knew I needed the break. The laundromat where some chick stole my clothes from a dryer, and the flophouse where I found her. Across the street from our house was the school playground. We had found a bat there once and decided to keep it for a pet, much to Mom's dismay. The bottle depot – I had cashed in there more then once. And, eerily, the phone booth where we often had to phone the police still stood on the same corner.

There wasn't anything romantic about our old neighbourhood. Along the drag, several old bars I had trolled as a kid had been bulldozed, except the York Hotel, which appeared as dismal and seedy as I remembered. Driving down memory lane, I felt the distance between then and now, but it was still the old neighbourhood.

Three months after I returned from Alaska, a letter arrived. It was from the young woman I had met in jail. Her name is Darlene, and this is her story.

As a child, Darlene had witnessed her mother being raped and beaten to death. Then she had to live at her father's house, where she was abused. By the time Darlene was twelve, she had started prostituting herself, using drugs and drinking in order to cope. She explained her eventual involvement with crime, and now she was doing her time. She was having difficulty in jail because she saw the man who murdered her mom on a regular basis. She prayed not to be resentful, but she couldn't help but hate him. She asked if I would be her mommy, because her mommy had cared like I did. She wrote, "I know there's a different way to live and you're living proof of that."

I was humbled, and fell to my knees in gratitude for everything I had survived because my life had inspired her not to give up. I wrote back to Darlene immediately, and told her I would be honoured to be her mommy, and I would do my best to be there for her from then on.

I phoned her one day, and she told me, "You're an angel in my eyes."

If only Darlene had known the strength she had given me. On the day her letter arrived, I was premeditating a drunk, feeling sorry for myself. Her life made a difference to me, as did mine to her, and as we wrote each other, our words were our reprieve, for a brief while.

A year later, Darlene was in a transition house. I sensed there was something wrong, so I phoned her there. When she answered, I said, "Hello Sweetie, it's Mom..." She was crying. "Are you okay?" I asked, and through her choked tears she told me that while she was on a day pass two weeks ago, two men had raped her. My adopted daughter so many miles away needed me, and there was nothing I could do but listen over the phone as she cried. I wanted to jump on a plane and rescue her, and then I wanted to kill those bastards.

We lost touch after that conversation, in spite of my efforts to find her. I've held onto the words of one of her letters, and pray, if it be the Creator's will for us to meet, let it be before her last wish. She wrote, "...I am dealing with a lot of my childhood memories right now (especially with my Mom's murder) also learning to love myself. That is so hard for me because I've always believed that I was insane because of all the shit I went through... Courage is walking through fears and facing the unknown, if you can make it, so can I... Even though we're very distant, I can feel your love surrounding me... you and I deserve the best that we can have. Whenever I die I want to put on my tombstone, 'Darlene died clean and sober,' if I know I died clean and sober, I will have accomplished everything in life... You're in my prayers and I love you too."

I think of Darlene always.

IN GOD'S TIME

The week after I received the first of several letters from Darlene in the mail, a previous employer contacted me to tell me about a conference he thought would be beneficial for me. I was unemployed at the time, and although I was looking for work, I was unwilling to work as a youth consultant. The conference was about providing workshops on sexual abuse, and he was willing to waive my fee and provide free room and board. I explained my reluctance to facilitate sexual abuse workshops because I felt I wasn't qualified. He assured me that the focus would remain on our own personal development as participants, not facilitators. I agreed to attend.

From the outset, I felt his passive-aggressive behaviour toward me: giving me the silent treatment, and speaking to me only when he felt obligated to. Apparently, I was being taught a lesson in control. I wondered why he had invited me in the first place, and on the second night, I confronted him. We argued head on. I told him that he was using our people's pain as a commodity, and I questioned his motives and told him to get off his high horse.

Needless to say, it didn't go over very well, and I found myself stranded, without gas money or a place to stay. I went to a twelve-step meeting that night, spinning out in my head. At the meeting, a lady took notice of me, and then sat beside me. I explained my circumstances when asked to share, and to my surprise, everyone donated gas money. Irene invited me to stay at her place for the night. I accepted, and then I leaned close to her as I whispered, "Am I okay?"

She held my hand. "Yes, you're okay," Irene reassured me as she looked me straight in my eyes, and from that moment on, she took care of me.

We drove to a restaurant for coffee afterward. I sat in a booth surrounded by five women, all with over five years of sobriety. The conversation led to sexual abuse issues and recovery. For the first time, in sobriety, I openly talked about my sexual abuse with strangers who empathetically listened to me. No one interrupted or offered advice, and though I heard what I was saying, I heard a child speaking.

I left my car at the restaurant and Irene drove me to her house. I sat in the back seat, a grown woman retreating into a child-like state of mind. I looked at my hands, wondering whose hands they were. When we arrived at her home, Irene made a comfortable bed for me on her couch. I fell into a deep sleep.

I find an abandoned old shack. My mom is with me but refuses to walk into the shack with me, so I leave her outside. I look around, but I don't know what I'm searching for. I hear a child's whimpering and a baby's raspy struggle to breathe. The shack is filthy, the floor covered with dirt, dust several centimetres thick, mouldy mucus filling the corners and countertops. My breathing quickens as my heart beats anxiously. I cautiously walk through one room and into another, following the whimpering. It is a bedroom. Before me is a crib, and in the crib lies a three-year-old girl and a toddler of eighteen months. They are barely alive.

I look back and scream for my mom to help. She ignores me as she stands at the door watching. I race into the larger room, find a white cloth, wet it with water and run back to the crib. I tenderly wipe the faces of the little girl and baby, wetting their dehydrated lips, and as their breathing returns to normal, I soothe them, assuring them that I will never leave them. I pick up the toddler and the girl and walk out of the shack. My mom is nowhere to be found, but I weep in relief that the babies are safe with me.

I woke crying.

Mesmerized by the dream, I thought about the night before, remembering how much I had disclosed to these women I didn't know, and then I became paranoid. Although I often referred to my sexual abuse when I spoke in workshops, this was the first time I had experienced my feelings. I wasn't telling a story.

I looked around Irene's living room. She had a comfortable home. Plants flourished in the sunlight near windows. Beige doilies complemented her end tables. There was a love seat opposite the couch, where I lay wrapped in a blanket. On the coffee table was a glass bowl filled with candy. There were family pictures everywhere: on her television, end tables, and hung on walls. The kitchen was crowded with a table, four chairs, and a matching cabinet, everything in its place.

Irene found me sitting on her couch, deep in thought. She made coffee and asked if I wanted breakfast. I said yes, and moved to her kitchen table. Feeling uncomfortable, I tried to redeem myself. "I really slipped off last night..."

"But you're okay now," Irene interrupted. "How do you want your eggs cooked?"

I gathered it wasn't necessary for me to explain what had happened.

As we ate breakfast, Irene told me about herself, and what it was like for her the first time she disclosed her sexual abuse to her psychologist. I listened, still raw and emotional, admiring how freely she spoke about the terror she experienced the first time she talked about what had happened to her as a child. I related to how she thought she would die if she ever told anyone, only to realize that she had to tell her secrets because they were preventing her from moving on in life.

Irene spoke without shame, remorse or self-pity, and she didn't come from a place of fear or resentment. She was forgiving of herself, and she said she prayed for her offender often, and in doing so, she no longer had to live with his guilt. She realized that she'd blamed herself for the sexual abuse, and this revelation became the turning point in reclaiming her voice. She realized how, for years, she had punished herself without being aware of what she was doing. Accepting that she had never had control over what had happened to her as a child released her from her offender's bondage, and later in life, her own self-bondage.

In Irene's opinion, "Everything happens in God's time when it comes to healing, and it's important to be patient with the process, and kind to yourself."

I held onto every word Irene said, and I knew by the feeling behind my belly button that she was being completely honest and real about her life. This appealed to me, and I wanted to be able to talk about my sexual abuse without being consumed with shame or fear. I wanted to experience the freedom she felt in her heart.

Someone knocked at her door. She looked at the clock, and remembered she was babysitting that morning for a girlfriend. Irene introduced me to Mavis and Sara, Mavis's eight-year-old daughter. As Mavis went over her schedule with Irene, Sara came to the table and sat across from me. She smiled, making me smile too. I watched Sara, in awe of her innocence. She was just a baby.

Irene came to the kitchen when Mavis left, poured herself another coffee, and noticed how mesmerized I was with Sara, and softly asked, "Is she an adult?"

I looked at Sara across from me. "No. She's just a baby." Tears streamed slowly down my face.

Irene quickly asked me another question, "Was it your fault?"

I couldn't contain myself. "No. I was just a child..." and I cried uncontrollably.

Irene handed me Kleenex and sent Sara to play in the living room, then sat across from me. "That's right, you were just a child. There was nothing you could do, and it isn't your fault."

A heavy grief weighed on my chest, making me nauseous. I asked Irene what was happening to me. She simply stated, "You're feeling." I understood: I was feeling the loss of my childhood, feeling the pain, feeling what I hadn't allowed myself to feel most of my life. I became terrified as the fuse in my memory blew, while my brain transferred mixed messages back and forth.

Feeling.

"You're so emotional!"

Don't feel.

It was real and it did happen.

"You always make such a big deal of everything!"

What I'm feeling is wrong.

Crying.

"You're so sensitive!"

Don't cry.

"The past is the past!"

My pain doesn't matter.

Irene let me cry without intervening, and for the first time in my life, I acknowledged my sexual abuse without shame. When I couldn't cry anymore, I excused myself and took a long, hot shower, mentally and emotionally fragile and exhausted.

After the shower, I caught a glimpse of myself in the mirror. Wiping the steam from the mirror; I stared at my face and then my body. I no longer felt numb from the waist down. I marvelled at how my vagina and uterus made me a woman, yet being sexually abused disconnected me from myself. I traced my scar with my finger. It remained as deep and formidable as when I received it.

I moved closer to the mirror, searching my dark brown eyes, which were bare without make-up, yet soft and alive. Then I flashed back to being nine years old, standing in front of the mirror. My budding breasts were bumps and I wanted them to be bigger, until I remembered that if they were bigger, Jake would touch me more, and then big boobs weren't so appealing.

I shivered at the memory.

Having regrouped, I looked at the woman staring back.

It's been such a long journey.

Sara was watching television as I folded the blankets Irene had made my bed with, and then we had another coffee. We talked through the events of the past twenty-four hours. I needed to compose myself. Irene reassured me. No, I wasn't losing my mind, and I didn't have to sentence myself to a prison of shame because of being sexually abused. My masochistic attitude made sense somehow, or at least it was beginning to.

Sara needed Irene's attention, so I asked Irene if she could take me to my car. I had to get going. At the restaurant, I found my car where we had left it the night before, and I thanked Irene for everything. She offered one suggestion, "Be kind to yourself and patient with the process of healing."

As we hugged good-bye, I knew I had made a turning point in my life by breaking my silence.

'CAUSE YOU'RE AN INDIAN

The drive back to Edmonton was filled with emotional residue, as the previous night's disclosure of sexual abuse brought to the forefront, with a fury, clichés of shame in my life.

I remembered incidents that made me uneasy in my skin and angered, powerless, because they were caused by being a Native woman. I could deal with my own issues, but I didn't know how to contend with what wasn't mine, attitudes that were projected onto me, for no other reason than because I'm an Indian.

I was working on a rig, as a cook's helper and camp attendant. After I sobered up, I needed the fast cash, so I returned to work in the service sector briefly. It had been years since I'd worked in an isolated environment. I was living in a narrow trailer dropped in the middle of Alberta, surrounded by trees, thick with mud on a rainy day and desolate of modern conveniences for miles.

One week in camp and several arguments with the cook later, I decided to join the boys for a Saturday night in town – play a little pool, drink a few Pepsis and watch people get drunk. What harm could there be in that? I knew who to avoid, and hung out with a young fellow, Trevor, who appeared harmless and naïve.

He told bad jokes and talked too much, but I didn't think he would try anything on me.

Much to my relief, Trevor wanted to sit alone with me, not join the already rowdy crew who watched us like hawks, laughing among themselves. They drank their beer fast, talked loud, played the jukebox, and occasionally looked over and winked at Trevor, then laughed more. Trevor didn't waste any time gulping his beer, anxious for that euphoric buzz I remembered. With my back against the wall, I decided not to play pool, feeling outnumbered. I was getting restless.

An hour passed, and Trevor's speech soon became incoherent slurs as he repeated jokes, still laughing at them whether I did or not. I felt uneasy as the night progressed, and the crowd became more restless. Maybe going out wasn't such a good idea after all. Trevor eventually staggered over to the table where most of the crew were seated. They roused him and then slapped him on the back. From where I was sitting, I couldn't hear their jovial remarks.

He managed to make his way back to our table, slumping into his seat, almost sliding off as he shyly looked over at me, then back at the boys. I sensed something was up and braced myself. With a cross-eyed plea, he attempted to say something, then stopped mid sentence. I watched him as he struggled to form another sentence, not knowing how to express what he wanted to say. Like a fool, I became concerned. I moved my chair closer to him, and suggested he spit out whatever was on his mind. He cautiously looked at me. Shrugging his shoulders, he sheepishly said, "The guys... well... they..."

I became impatient. "Just say it," I demanded.

"They say you're not a real Canadian till you've had an Indian woman, and, you know, you're an Indian..."

"So you want me to have sex with you?" I asked in bewilderment.

"Well, I mean, if you don't mind."

I couldn't believe what I was hearing. "You mean to tell me, all these years I've been with Immigration and didn't even know it?" I asked sarcastically.

Trevor's eyes pleaded with me, "No disrespect, but everyone I know has had an Indian. Well?"

"No, Trevor," I firmly replied, "I will not have sex with you, even if it means you will not officially be a Canadian!"

"Just thought I'd ask," he explained. "The guys have been ribbing me since you got to camp." I looked over and saw most of the men laughing as they watched us. I got up and headed directly for their boss. The laughter stopped. I demanded to be taken back to camp. Their boss knew what was going on and agreed to drive me back. I lasted another day in camp before an all-out screaming match with the cook and an argument with their boss sent me packing.

Until then, I had never realized that men expect casual sexual favours from me because I'm an Indian, although once I had thought about it, it was obvious.

When I was only twenty and still drinking, I decided to go out one night to a trendy nightclub in Saskatoon for a night of dancing. A ruggedly handsome young man noticed me in the bar. This tall blond pretty-boy introduced himself, and then he bought me a beer. We talked and danced all night.

I didn't get it. I didn't think I was his type, but I was at ease with him, and he seemed like a nice guy. He was in his first year of agriculture at the university, new to Saskatoon and city living. Although he was with a group of buddies from university, he hung around me all night. When closing time came, he offered to drive me home, and I accepted. Once we got to my place, he parked his truck, and then leaned over and kissed me. I thanked him for the ride and offered to get together again. Writing my phone number on my cigarette pack, I handed it to him. He took it and said, "To be honest, the guys and I made bets on who could get laid, and that's the only reason I hung around with you tonight. I'm sorry. It's just someone said you looked easy, you know, 'cause you're Indian. But you're really a nice person and I can't do this. And I probably won't phone you so... see you around."

I stood in shock as I watched his truck drive away, feeling like I'd been punched in the stomach.

"You look easy, you know, 'cause you're Indian..."

Walking down most city streets guarantees a proposition. I've stopped counting the johns who honk their horns, then pull over and wait for me to jump in their vehicle. Some are more polite than others. One young man exposed himself as he flagged me to join him. Others lean over, anxious to open the passenger door as I pass by.

At first, I walked taller in an effort to ignore the looks and remarks. After a while, the lewd comments and looks of disdain or open desire bordered on ridiculous and progressed to verbal assault. Initially, I reacted with rage, swearing and screaming like a madwoman, offering my middle finger in response to the directions they claimed to seek.

These incidents still affect me much the same as when I was a child growing up on the drag, and at home, when some predator propositioned me. Nausea grips my gut. I become horrified, embarrassed, and then angry.

During the five-hour drive from Lethbridge to Edmonton, I screened a bad black-and-white movie of the life of me, an Indian woman. As Edmonton's city skyline of lights invited me into its electrical orbit I was saddened by how some things haven't changed since the days of old Fort Edmonton.

The Indian women birthed the Métis Nation. Their skilful hands kept their husbands' fires strong, hunting for and feeding them. After their children's fathers had done their part to forge a new land, many renounced their descendants and walked away. After all,

Indian women are not meant for marriage in the Christian way, pro-claimed a Steward – they are meant to sustain our Hudson's Bay employees in the cold of minus thirty degrees, so if you please, dispose of her, your Indian wife, she is of no use, now that the country is open for settlers to arrive, with good Christian wives. Trade the Indian woman at the post, where you boast that she is good only when placed on her back, so good in fact, we can no longer tell an Indian from the half-breeds in need. How can you claim to love the Indian woman? By virtue of her skin, marriage to her would be somewhat of a sin. Let it be known, Indian women are expendable and available for Clerks who know little of the value and worth of a lady, and surely, these Indian women are unfit to fall into this category. Set them out-side of the walls of our Forts, then only allow the Indian women in to entertain our gentlemen, as is their place. Otherwise, do not dis-grace yourselves, or our Company, by showing their faces among our Lords. These heathens can bear your children, if need be, but no longer at the cost of the Hudson's Bay Company. These Indian women are meant for sexual gratification, for our men are weary, and our ladies so few, therefore, Indian women shall have to do...

ON THE BACKROADS
OF INDIAN COUNTRY

Comfort came in the form of a little man I loved and his innocent need, as a child, and reliance on me, his mother, to care for him. I couldn't afford self pity or depression. I had to be there for him. Regardless of what life hurled my way, in spite of my own healing and personal issues, meals had to be provided, clothes washed, playtime and bedtime had to be tended to. Mending my wounds could wait – I had to suck it up and be available, ignoring the dam of tears that emerged as my heart melted. I had to be patient with the process of healing, as Irene had suggested.

Joint custody was stressful because I was never permanently employed, which meant raising Matthew on welfare when he lived with me. As Matthew grew, I became fearful and frustrated by not knowing if I was parenting right. I had no basis in healthy parenting to compare it to. My only option was not raising him the way I had been raised. I knew more about what *not* to do than what *to* do.

One day, in my aggravation, I said to Matthew, "Look, I don't know how to do this... how to be a good mom... a good parent..."

Matthew's big brown eyes consoled me as he said quite empathetically, "Feed me three times a day, make sure I go to bed on time and get to school."

His six-year-old simplicity helped me realize that as long as I did my best to cover the basics, I could figure things out as we went.

I made him lunch for two in grade one, encouraging him to share his food with anyone who might not have a lunch. One day he came home delighted because the teacher had asked the kids to place their extra food on a shelf so that others could help themselves. But when I asked him how he liked grade one and he said, "It's boring, all we do is draw and colour," I was shocked because I had felt the same way. I decided to place him in a special school for gifted children when he got older. I wanted him to be challenged at a level he was capable of.

Hamburger soup and bannock wasn't our staple meal; it was a treat. Much like dried meat and fish, both were savoured when we had them. We snuggled while reading stories or watching our favourite programs, and I never allowed the television to occupy his every moment at home.

I purged my past quietly to myself, and all that mattered were our hugs good morning, good night, and several more for extra measure in between. We talked silly often, and I marvelled at his every comment. Matthew's two small steps kept up with my long stride when we went for walks, and now and then, the claw – my hand – chased him, tickling his tummy when it caught him. So it began – my little man and I started growing up together.

Shared custody of Matthew kept life interesting. I managed to remain stable for the first half of Matthew's years with me in grades one and three, but mid way through I sent him back to Dan because I had to move for employment, or because I got involved in the insanity of a relationship. By grade five, Dan informed me that Matthew was to remain for a full year or he would assume sole custody. I settled down as much as I could while Mathew lived with me and kept him for a full term. Losing Matthew again was not something I was going to allow, simply because of my inability, at that time, to get grounded in life.

By my mid-twenties, I had sought therapy with a psychologist in Edmonton. Unravelling the knot in my soul wasn't a lone passage. There were milestones along the way, and people who loved me when I couldn't love myself.

My spiritual foundation had been laid at a prayer sweat years earlier. I was twenty-one the first time I attended a sweat. My friend Mary had been going to prayer sweats for years, and I was curious, as well as anxious, when I agreed to go. I wasn't raised with any teachings on Aboriginal culture or ceremonies, so it was all new to me.

The sweat was on a reserve, and when we arrived, I remained quiet. Not wanting to be disrespectful, I listened and watched. The home of the family holding the sweat was inviting and warm as everyone shook hands. I found a place to sit in the living room. In the kitchen, a large table was filled with a feast of food. It was apparent that Mary was well known, and everyone was happy to see her.

A young man walked in and said the sweat was ready. Mary brought me to the bedroom to change into our flannel nightgowns while the men went outside. Mary told me about her first sweat, saying that when it was over, everyone shook her hand, smiling lovingly while some were laughing. She didn't realize her mascara had smeared during the sweat and that she looked like a racoon. I made sure I washed my face before we went in.

I was scared, and it was hot, and by the time the second round was over, I couldn't handle any more and crawled out, hyperventilating. My hands were knotted, and I could barely breathe. I curled up on the earth like a drowned muskrat having a seizure. I couldn't go back in to finish the last two rounds. After I caught my breath and was able to stand, I changed and waited for the sweat to end.

I was embarrassed at not being able to withstand the heat, yet it was the most beautiful experience I'd ever had. I wanted more, just not at the moment. I knew I had to wait until I was better prepared, now that I knew what happened at a sweat. It was healing for me, and since then, I have found spiritual refuge in attending prayer sweats. They have helped me clear my mind and ground myself. I came to experience sweats as an extremely intimate union between self and spirit. This empowered me.

I soon found myself on the backroads of Indian country, on the powwow trail, remaining close with another friend who was a fancy dancer. Carmen grew up with her culture, and at the time, she was my mentor.

I was never inclined to dance at powwows. I figured that Dene people have drum dances too, and they're different, that's all. The Dene drummers have a distinct, unique rhythm and beat that enraptures me. The songs are a soulful symphony of quick high pitches that rise from the depth of each singer as he sings in his Dene language. One song can honour the land, another ancestors. They make legends come alive in spiritual eloquence and synchronicity, while as many as twelve drummers sing the story into life.

As the northern lights appear beneath a starry sky, people gravitate toward a fire and begin dancing around it, clockwise, in a circle. Hopping in formation, bodies respond to the rhythm. The shoulders loosen and shake to the beat of the drum. Gyrating hips bounce as feet shimmy over the earth. The singers and dancers blend their energy like flames crackling off fire. As the heat intensifies, the motions escalate into a frenzied fever of celebration as natural as the wilderness. We dance late into the night.

While dancing, I think of my family and friends, and the harder I dance, the more entranced I become as I visualize our ancestors dancing with us. I dance in memory of the days when they still held tea dances in Dog Head.

Dene dancers dance without full regalia, unlike powwow dancers. We dress casually, although sometimes dancers adorn themselves with traditional beaded vests, jackets or moccasins. Though Dene dancers aren't as visually captivating as powwow dancers, they are as vibrant and energetic.

One night at a powwow, I was buying a coffee at a concession, when someone tapped me on the shoulder. I turned around and looked down. Standing there was a women's traditional dancer, about four foot two. "You got a husband?" she asked.

I looked around. She was talking to me, so I replied, "No. Just a coffee."

She looked me up and down and said, "My brodder wants to meet you," then pointed her lips toward a truck. I looked over and saw no one. She told me, "Come with me – he's over dare." I followed out of curiosity.

She introduced me to a young grass dancer who was changing out of his outfit. He turned red, pink, and white and then ran off, once he'd got his pants on. She shook her head, muttering something in Cree. I walked away with my coffee.

The following winter at a round dance, the same young grass dancer joined me with an older man, one on my left, the other on my right. While we were dancing, the young man leaned into me and whispered, "It's my odder brodder who wants to meet you," pointing his lips toward the older man on my right.

I danced all night and managed to escape being snagged. I caught on fast.

Attending powwows, round dances and prayer sweats became a way of life. I met Elders, sisters and brothers, and then powwows became a yearly reunion. Dancers, drum groups and those who sit in the bleachers gathered, some to watch, others to participate. I watched, or danced during an intertribal, unless Dene drummers performed, and then I danced the Dene way.

Throughout the years, there were people I especially enjoyed meeting again. Dwayne was one such person, and as it had been when we first met, he remained a brother, friend and confidant. We'd catch up with life, and often we both had a lot of living to reflect on since we had last seen each other. There was no greater reminder of the change in my life than visiting with Dwayne. I still lost myself in his eyes and in his stories. Many people had come and gone since we'd met, yet few remained as significant to me as he did. Beneath the arbour we'd sit and listen to the drummers, watch the dancers, and carry on with our socializing.

My spirit became alive on the trail, in Indian Country. On the backroads, you spend a lot of time setting camp, and tearing down camp, enjoying fresh air, joking, laughing, teasing and, everyone's favourite pastime, teepee creeping, which also requires a lot of time in a tent. If that wasn't enough, between powwows there were miles and miles of country to admire, mountains, rivers, and different reserves.

There was a time when Indians were not allowed to leave reserve lands without a permit – they were prisoners. Their nomadic lifestyle of hunting and living freely on the land was restricted. Then, Indians were given rations, which were provided by an Indian agent, and if he didn't want to distribute the rations, he wouldn't. This often caused starvation among the Indians.

During a grand entry at a powwow, the flags are carried into the arbour, usually by veterans, followed by dignitaries and honoured guests. Watching veterans is especially moving because, during World War II, veterans returning home did not receive the same recognition as white veterans. In fact, many treaty Indians lost their status when they went to war, and when they came home, federal law kept Indians on reserve.

The Canadian government began trying to outlaw Indian ceremonies and dances through the Indian Act in 1884, and did not officially lift the ban for seventy-five years. As I watched the dancers, I considered how, in spite of everything, a new generation of beautiful, colourful and strong dancers now performed so proudly. It is an amazing sight to behold, as though the people are awakening from a great sleep to celebrate life.

Then I thought about those who weren't watching alongside me and the hundreds of other people beneath the arbour, the brothers and sisters in jails, on the street, and I'd say a prayer for them during the opening ceremony. I know what it is like to be homeless, hungry and hopeless.

During my spiritual quest, I was doctored by a medicine man. He gave me medicines to drink over three days while he prayed for me, with me, and over me as I wrestled with my own demons. Then one morning, the medicine man woke and said the grandfathers had told him to give me my spirit name, Wandering Earth Spirit Woman, which describes me perfectly. This name reflects my spirit and my destiny in life. When he finished doctoring me, he gave me more medicine to drink for four days and said, "My girl, your spirit is bruised. Drink your medicine and rest. Don't do anything else. Just take care of you."

I went home intending to follow his instructions. The problem was my body ached from my head to my feet, inside out. I have a high tolerance for pain, but I couldn't handle it. I went to emergency and, naturally, the intern couldn't find anything wrong with me, so he sent me home, still in pain. At home, I phoned the medicine man. He said he'd be right over. When he arrived, I was affectionately reprimanded for going to the hospital and not listening to his instructions. "I told you to rest and stay home and drink your medicines."

"My body hurts, everywhere," I snapped back.

He said he knew. "I told you, your spirit is bruised. Your spirit is healing. Think about what you've been through as a child, and that is what the medicine is healing, your spirit."

I understood. I just wished he had explained it to me before. We prayed and I dutifully drank my medicine and went to sleep for four days, waking only to drink my medicine, go the bathroom, and eat. Irene's words came back: "Everything happens in God's time when it comes to healing, so be patient with the process and be kind to yourself."

This medicine man assisted me on my journey of healing. He did not heal me – the medicines from Mother Earth and the Creator did. This medicine man humbly made himself available to the Creator and devoted his life to his gift of healing people through the Creator and medicines provided by Mother Earth. He himself understood he was merely the instrument.

Crow was loud, and full of himself, but quiet eagle soared high above, close to the sun. Eagle used his beautiful voice to give thanks, or to acknowledge and bless his relations. Eagle didn't need to be noticed, so his spirit was free; crow needed to be noticed, so he was too busy to notice anyone but himself.

Then coyote came along, and being the trickster that he is, one day he tricked eagle; eagle was watching crow caw in a tree. Coyote tricked eagle into believing he needed to be noticed like crow. And eagle got full of himself, like crow, and rather than soaring high in the sky, eagle came down to earth and sat in a tree, hurting all the four-legged animals with his loud screech as he cawed to be noticed.

All the animals left the valley because eagle was so full of himself that he was a nuisance. Everyone left but a lone crow sitting on man in a field, and as each day passed, even the insects had to leave because eagle was now flying over the valley cawing loudly, scaring everyone.

Eagle decided he needed a wife, he asked man for crow's hand in marriage – after all, crow was faithful to him and waited every day for him to fly by. Man did nothing and said nothing when eagle asked for crow's hand in marriage, so after the fourth day of asking, eagle decided to take crow from man and attacked man and accidentally killed crow too.

Now eagle had no one as he cried and cawed in the tree.

Meanwhile, high in the sky, eagle's real wife heard an awful sound, which sounded familiar. It sounded like her missing husband! So she followed the noise and found her husband in a tree, crying and cawing. She landed on the branch next to him and asked where he'd gone and why he was crying.

Eagle had to think about it. Then he realized what had happened. Coyote had tricked him into believing he needed to be noticed and admired like crow, who was always noticed, but only because he was loud. Because of this moment of envy, coyote gave eagle crow's ego. Eagle returned to the skies with his wife, laughing at himself all the way. And he never wished to be anyone but himself again, not even for a second.

Coyote had a good laugh too, and all the animals returned to the valley.

You see, I wanted to be a crow once, until I realized that I'm a wolf.

Just a story, that's all.

A LOST GENERATION

Time is the only healer, especially when it comes to family, and time was all I had. My sisters and I weren't as close as we once were. Everyone was getting on with life, work, children and careers. I had created boundaries with Mom because I couldn't take watching her in her alcoholism, and, as painful as it was, I had to remind myself that I wasn't responsible for her. It took a long time to understand that I never had been.

Learning the difference between being controlling and caring for someone was critical. Trying to control someone else is like trying to navigate a dingy in a typhoon – impossible. Until I accepted my mom's alcoholism, and mine, I wasn't able to recognize my compulsion to rescue her instead of accepting her and loving her for who she is.

I wanted to bridge the emotional distance between us, or at least understand the void. I knew there was more to her life than what I was aware of, so I started exploring her history when I was fortunate enough to meet someone who was researching residential schools.

While assisting Dr. Carney of the University of Alberta, whose research was specifically with northern residential schools,

I became aware of the links between parent and child that were almost severed, and of the tragedies of family and community genocide. I finally saw myself as part of the big picture. An eagle soaring high, I caught a glimpse beyond the clouds and grey skies, far beyond the silver lining, to an elusive place of clarity and silence, a place where all that exists on earth remains timeless, and there is nothing but space. I found peace. I found forgiveness. I found myself embracing my mom, my son and me; we three generations became linked, in my heart.

As swiftly as I soared high, finally comprehending why I couldn't make the link before, I fell further and further into an abyss of rage and confusion. Integrating truth, history and humanity landed me flat on my ass, overwhelmed. Distraught and challenged, I tried to open my narrow mind, much like wrenching a locked door open with an iron rod. It was hard because I had to look beyond myself once again, only to realize that it isn't about me. It's history.

In 1862, the Holy Angels Convent and residential school opened. The Grey Nuns ran the mission.

I interviewed several women who attended the Holy Angels Mission in Fort Chipewyan, the second of three generations that went through the mission, and through that process I came to know my mom. They didn't speak of her directly; in fact, she was never mentioned. Yet they did speak of her through experiences they had shared in their lives, a pivotal point that had incomprehensible consequences. These interviews were especially close to home for me because many of the women I interviewed were the same women who babysat me, and whose children I grew up with.

Each woman I interviewed had her own personal story, but the similarities in character, behaviour and choices were undeniable. They all struggled with issues of parenting, alcoholism and drug abuse, depression and an inability to conform or function in society in a productive manner. For the most part, those who could function did so under tremendous stress.

They shared a generic profile: difficulty with intimacy in relationships, whether with a spouse or with their children and families. Many had no desire to return to their communities as a result of memories of hardship and the loneliness they had experienced in the residential school. Some lost their children to Social Services at some point in their lives because they didn't know how to parent. Those whose children remained in their lives had limited parenting skills. They provided the best they could – the basics.

I thought about Mom, remembering how I struggled for her physical affection and love, for her to take notice of me. I dug deep into my memory and couldn't remember being held or hugged by her unless I instigated it, and when I did, it was a shrug more than a hug, as if she wondered why I would need her to hold me. It was more of a brush off, until I stopped seeking her affection. I thought about the days when being fed was more than I could hope for, when life was about survival and drinking, violence and neglect, abuse and rejection. As I thought about these childhood events and times with my mom, it hit me: How often had she needed to be held too? Did she learn *not* to be affectionate? Was showing affection and being affectionate potentially dangerous? Had she been as lonely as I was as a child? Did she cry for her mom too, her dad, my Grandpa Jonas – anyone? Did someone hold her? Could she escape those dormitory walls through a hole in the wall as we had as children? Were there ever times she could hope to crawl out to seek comfort and safety?

I pondered these questions as I talked to these women. Some were affected by the experience of residential schools more than others. One woman had difficulty leaving her apartment, and feared human contact, experiencing anxiety attacks in public places. She had had several nervous breakdowns throughout her life, yet when talking about the Holy Angels Mission, she was articulate and consciously aware of how she had been affected by the experience. She fully comprehended her inability to parent or bond with her children, and how as a result, her mother had raised them.

Other women appeared to be made of tougher material, yet they were not as candid about their experiences in residential school, and were unwilling to disclose how it had affected their lives. They minimized what had occurred to such a degree that they made it sound pleasant, only reflecting on the good times while not allowing painful memories to surface.

Good times: Learning to sew, cook, crochet, knit, garden and care for and defend other children. Speaking French while being beaten if they spoke Cree or Chipewyan. Boys learned carpentry, farming, and how to read and write in a foreign language. Everyone learned how to perform manual labour, presumably to serve the larger society when leaving the mission. The nuns and priests were ill equipped to teach anything, and not educated enough to teach sciences or math during that era.

Many referred to the beatings and malicious ridicule they were subjected to by the priests and nuns. The food was more suitable for a dog, in their opinion: rotten fish and porridge.

They had to pray from morning to night, and were tormented and scorned as sinners when anyone acted out or rebelled. Rules were strictly enforced. Girls were not allowed to speak to boys and vice versa, whether they were related or not, and if they were caught, the retribution was shameful and horrific. They spoke of missing siblings and parents, and not being allowed to be with their families but for a short time during the summer months. Their isolation and loneliness were referred to more than anything, until being unloved and un-nurtured became normal.

Many walked away from residential schools with learned abusive behaviour, while internalizing the abrasive attitudes of nuns and priests, like clones acting out what was done unto them. Beneath their defensive walls were hurt, lonely children who ached for the love of their families, and the familiarity of their language.

In the hierarchy of abuse, older kids tormented the younger, behaviour that traced itself back to the priests and nuns.

The nuns had a regimen of cleaning that was used as method of punishment. I remember cleaning our house growing up: it had to be done thoroughly and perfectly or Mom twisted off. I never understood her behaviour until I listened to these women speak about their experiences in the Holy Angels Mission.

As I listened to each woman share her history with me, I was given a picture of what Mom had gone through, just enough for me to remove the wedge in my heart, which hadn't budged most of my life. Mom was tough, and my defence against her prevented us from bonding. She hadn't bonded with her own mom. Grandma Anne was ill with tuberculosis during Mom's childhood and was in hospital a lot.

Many Aboriginal children arrived at residential schools in good health, only to test positive for tuberculosis within a few years because of overcrowding in the schools. Many tuberculosis survivors carried the disease home.

Mom didn't raise me to speak the Dene language because she was beaten and ridiculed when she spoke it in the mission. She once told me, "I wanted you to have a better life than being ridiculed for being an Indian." When her grandmothers visited her in her dreams, speaking to her of medicines and prayers in Dene, Mom went to the nuns, who told her she was the devil's spawn, and then she had to pray for forgiveness. Her ancestral links were attacked and her spirituality condemned. Mom denied her natural psychic ability, refusing to acknowledge her keen intuition as a seer as a result of what had happened to her.

Later, Mom chastised me for participating in sweats and tried to shame me for my curiosity about Indian ceremony. "That wasn't how I was raised!" she exclaimed.

When she calmed down, she spoke to me of things she sensed too, as if to say "You don't know anything." Then in another breath she demanded I give *it* back to my youngest sister Tania, the seventh daughter of the seventh daughter, for whom *it* was intended, *it* being my psychic ability and intuition.

It confused me as much as excited me when she admitted to her intuitive ability in one breath and then in another denied it, demanding I honour our hereditary order. "It wasn't supposed to go to you! It was meant for your sister! Not you!"

As usual, without even knowing or trying, I managed to wrong her. If I had known what I was supposed to do in order to do right by her, I would have done it, but the brimstone in her eyes told me to let it be. I understood she wasn't raised with ceremony, and her prayers, however heartfelt, had once been a form of punishment. Yet I know she believes in Spirit, in God. I know she prays.

I also began to understand how our inherent ties to the land were our saving grace. The land is for her what it is for me, the tie that binds us. Living on the land with Grandpa Jonas and being raised by her grandmother when she was home is where her strength came from. The spirit of the land, like the spirit of our grandmothers, is not broken. There is spirit world, and there is earth, and in between is history in the making.

These women who shared their experiences with me, of their lives in the Holy Angels Mission, repaired a rip between Mom and me. Mom moved on in her life, away from the nightmares and neglect of the mission, leaving behind the life of a trapper's daughter, and divorcing herself from being a young wife, and then as a single mom in Edmonton, trying to fit in while running from the one thing no one can escape: history.

This small handful of women are symbolic of thousands of others whose stories are silenced but for statistics and surveys that diminish their individual lives. They are human beings, not numbers.

I remember the day I stood eye to eye against my mom, demanding to know why she wanted to drink herself to death. We were arguing with our chests slammed against each other in rage as she shouted, "If I want to die drunk, that's my fucking business!" I walked away feeling rejected by my mom's defiance against my plea for her to sober up. Since interviewing these women, I understood it was Mom's right to act in any form of resistance to her past that she chose.

She was five years old when she was legally placed in the Holy Angels Mission until she was sixteen. This was an institution where molesting children behind closed doors appeared to be normal, and condoned through deathly silence, much like it had been with me. I wondered if the children ever talked about the abuse among themselves, and how many children wept silently in the cold dormitories night after night, children isolated from families, parents and communities. Who would have had the courage to tell anyone about the abuse? Was there anyone they could have turned to, other than those who were abusing them?

I remembered the ghost stories.

The ones that say that within the mission walls, nuns aborted babies which are buried there. As a child listening to these stories, I didn't believe them, but now I wonder what in God's name happened in the Holy Angels Mission?

I thought about a conversation I had with Mom several years after I sobered up. "Mom, I know you know what Jake did to us when we were children, and I thought, if anyone hurt Matthew the way Jake hurt us, I'd want to kill them. I realize now, you must have lived in fear to have allowed what happened to us to happen without protecting us."

Mom replied calmly, and without excuse, "I feared for my life every day."

"I know, Mom, and I want you to know, I don't blame you, and I forgive you. I know you lived your life in fear..." Long before you met Jake, I thought silently to myself. "I love you, Mom."

"I love you too," she offered sincerely.

There was nothing left to say. All my life I had waited for this one moment of truth between us. I understood how immature it was of me to have any expectations of her to parent me at all. This freed me, although not without grieving my mom, as a daughter who never knew her as a parent. I sensed grieving the loss of my childhood was only part of the process, as my emotional canal got deeper with each passage of history revealed. I realized that the disturbing cycles of abuse and neglect are cohesive to Canadian history and genocide of Aboriginal people, for the establishment of Canada.

I've spent my life missing Mom. As a child, my loneliness was innocent and natural. I wanted my mommy. It was that simple. Eventually, I realized that to be held and loved was too much to hope for, and all I had left was an aching curiosity about what it would be like to be loved by her as a mother, rather than to take care of her as a daughter.

Eventually my resentment and anger slammed the door shut and I wasn't willing to open it for years. When I made attempts to, a Do Not Enter sign was prominently displayed. So I've settled for peeking through the keyhole, catching glimpses of her in secret while witnessing her humanity.

Mom was living in Fort McMurray when I arrived unexpectedly one morning. She was drinking and frying potatoes, standing over her stove in her barren kitchen, which had only a table and chairs. Her countertop was empty of trinkets and kitchenware. I asked how she was, restraining myself from hugging her. I never knew if my attempts to show affection would be blocked, so I got into the habit of scanning her mood first and reacting accordingly. It was always better to be safe than bitten by rejection.

She was casual toward me, though her eyes lit up when she saw me, which was a satisfactory moment of acknowledgement and enough to make me feel welcome. I perked up and asked how she'd been. She mischievously said, "I'm cooking for your brother." I don't have a brother, but, playing along, I asked where my brother was. "Sitting in the living room." Smiling to herself, she was obviously pleased with her game. I peeked around the corner to see a grey-haired old man sitting on the couch. He looked sickly and thin.

Her living room was also bare but for the necessities: a couch, a television on a small table and an armchair. Mom apologized for not being able to offer me anything. She didn't even have coffee, and in her home, there was no greater offence than not being able to offer a guest a cup of coffee at the very least. Not wanting her to feel bad, I was quick to tell her that I had just finished breakfast.

She filled a plate with fried potatoes and brought them to the old man, who ate feverishly. When he finished he told her that he had to go, to which Mom responded, "You're not going anywhere!" I sensed his discomfort with me there, so I told her that I had things to do and would return later in the day. She made me promise to come back, so I gave her a time and left.

When I returned, the old man was gone, and Mom explained he was homeless; he'd had polio and was a chronic alcoholic. She took him in to make sure he had a meal and a warm place to sleep now and again. She told me that he hadn't always been like this. He held three university degrees and was once successfully employed and married. One night when he was driving drunk, he killed a boy in a car accident. He never got over the incident, ending up where he is now.

It was forty below in the freezing wind when she had gone searching for him the night before, to find him passed out near a snow bank by a hotel. Relieved to find him, she had brought him home for the night. The day I went to visit her, she was frying up her last bit of food for him: potatoes.

I sat in amazement as I listened to Mom tell the story of this man – my brother – knowing few people would open their homes as she had for her friend, or bother to search for him in forty below weather. I visited her for the day and forgot about my problems, or what I thought were problems, proud of Mom and moved by her act of compassion. I savour that day in my memory, and what her kindness meant to one old man.

During another visit, I arrived at her house unexpectedly again. It was late at night, and she was drunk. I didn't know what to do, so I sat with her as she talked and cried over her losses in life, until I couldn't stay awake. I asked to stay for the night and she insisted I sleep on her bed.

I was lying in her bed as she sat alone in the kitchen, talking to herself and crying aloud, triggering childhood memories in me as I listened to her. Then she got up and came down the hall, toward the bedroom. Afraid she wanted to wake me to visit with her, I pretended to be asleep as she staggered into the bedroom, holding my breath as she came toward the bed and stood over me, watching me sleep. Mumbling under her breath, I heard her cooing, as only a mother does while watching her child sleep.

She sniffed the air, whispering to herself about how musty and stale the room smelled. She went to the bathroom, then came back again. This time, she sprayed the bedroom with her favourite drugstore perfume, just so I wouldn't have to sleep amid stale air. Her act of consideration moved me to tears.

I'd wasted so many years focusing on what was wrong in our relationship and on the hard times that I couldn't get past the pain to realize what Mom had taught me. These incidents are what I consider the defining moments of a person's character, and Mom became my greatest teacher of human compassion, despite our relationship.

We remain distant, and I still have a difficult time watching her in her alcoholism. She continues to push me away with her abusive behaviour, but I know she loves me, in her own way. I know she cares.

I didn't attend the Holy Angels Mission. I wasn't one of thousands of children over four generations who were forced to. Then again, I didn't have to attend: What Mom, Dad and Grandma learned – the good, bad and indifferent – was passed on to me anyway. I remain a survivor of generational indoctrination and abuse. But what did remain intact, in spite of history, is the strength of my spirit. I am not broken. I am grieving a lost generation.

She wore a torn, weathered blanket of shame, every stitch sewn by a sworn nun, fitted blanket, custom-made second skin, numbered and made to fit any Indian. Her raw skin itched of scattered thorns pressed into her fabric of penance and prayers, shattering a rosary in her grip. Reciting dawn to dusk made her forlorn, on her knees ripped open scabs of scorn, bleeding beneath her mission blanket now barely covered wounds hidden. Docile in a dormitory prison, among another generation of fear-reddened children, who are risen, as some are wakened to be taken quietly down a corridor of nightmares, into a child's worst fears. Released from her cage, chanting voices challenged true freedom, struggling to survive trauma, creating the stage of her drama. One generation after, I submitted to her, mission blanket in hand. Mission blanket, I shall hold vigil for the spirits you stole, baring my brown skin, covered no more, burning the mission blanket I once wore.

GRANDPA JONAS
JOURNEYS TO THE TEA DANCE

When I was twenty-seven, it was Matthew's year with Dan. I'd adjusted as best as I could to our arrangement, yet when he was away, I struggled with learning how to live in my own skin. Calm days came more frequently, with chaos close behind. Loneliness crept into every corner of my suite and resided with me, along with the insanity of my thoughts.

I ended another relationship because of violence – my violence. On the night it ended, I was curled up in a ball on the floor in my kitchen, crying and wondering why the voices of my mom and dad screamed in my head. I knew I was losing my mind. My boyfriend walked out with a bleeding face and broken glasses, and as I sat on the floor, I could not delete the scenes of Mom attacking Jake, or Dad yelling. In between their violence was me, sitting on the floor, after a bloodbath I'd created, as a small voice tried to tell me to stop and I couldn't.

I described this scene over and over to my psychologist, desperately trying to understand why I couldn't stop the rage, struggling to explain what had happened, what triggered the violence, and in the end, it didn't matter. What mattered was what I did, sober, and there was nothing he had done to provoke me to the extremes I had reached. It wasn't the first time I had been violent in a relationship, but it was the first time I tried to seek answers and get help. If the "ugly pills" of intimacy weren't enough to keep me single, it would appear that fear of my violence would.

In the midst of my questionable sanity, and trying to build a productive life without a blueprint, I received a phone call. Grandpa Jonas had passed away in Fort McMurray. Everything stopped. All I did was cry; there was nothing left in me afterward. I went into robotic motion and packed and then made arrangements to go home for the funeral.

The whole family attended Grandpa's funeral in Fort Chipewyan, and as sad as the occasion was, it was good to be home. I was happy to see people I had grown up with. It had been years since I had been back. I was still drinking when I had left, and my lifestyle had changed dramatically. It was a fresh reminder of how far I'd come, in spite of how insane I felt at times.

Being home for the funeral was filled with memories, good times and bad. When I thought of Grandpa, I remembered how his eyes held a mischievous glint that made us children laugh and forget whatever ached our hearts. I remembered the soulful, reassuring way he looked at me. No matter what, I knew it would be okay because he was there.

The only time I heard him raise his voice was when he yelled for us to go to bed, or when he said *drinking is no good* in Chipewyan. He remained proud and stubborn, refusing to speak English throughout his life unless he wanted to tease us; then he made an effort to speak in broken English, only to watch us react with giggles and surprise. He was someone we could depend on, and his actions made it clear that he loved us more than we knew.

I remember him stoking the fire in his two-room shack, where we all lived, and I mean all of us – ten to twelve people when we were all there. Most of us were young, so the adults delegated sleeping space on the couch and the two beds in the bedroom. I still don't know how we did it.

Grandpa Jonas was the first to wake, and he made sure the fire was going strong in the woodstove. Early each morning he would be outside chopping wood, piling it inside, warming water, and waiting for the shack to bustle with us girls as we tripped over each other while waiting for our turn on the frozen and often seatless honey bucket during winter months.

One evening, four of us girls were piled in one bed, fighting over space, blankets, and a piece of a pillow. With my head finally comfortable, I was just about asleep when a mouse ran over my head and almost got caught in my hair. My blood-curdling scream made everyone jump out of bed. I bounced up and down, shaking my head in a craze. The mouse dropped, and my miniature assailant ran out of the room as the rest of the girls turned the shack upside down, searching for the mouse and screaming every time someone saw it, afraid it would rampage in our bed all night. The mouse escaped.

Grandpa Jonas had a good laugh that night.

Mom said he was getting senile as he grew older; he spoke to children playing in the hills, telling them to be careful, but Mom saw no children there. But I believe he saw children, though they may have been spirits, perhaps of his own children. He and my late grandma Anne had had twelve children, and only four survived tuberculosis.

I wish I had asked Grandpa Jonas about his life. Now our family's oral history has left with him. It saddened me that he died in the hospital in Fort McMurray because I know he wanted to be at home in Fort Chipewyan, to feel the land once more and to see Lake Athabasca, and then say farewell to his relations.

I found comfort in knowing that Grandpa Jonas was taking the journey to the big tea dance, where his ancestors would greet him as he crossed over the lake in a canoe. Together, they would celebrate, and watch over us from spirit world, then dance among the northern lights.

I returned to Edmonton after the funeral.

There was more to my heritage than I realized, and I took it upon myself to research our family, especially after I learned of the Holy Angels Mission. I was proud to learn that my great-grandfather, Chief Laviolette, had signed Treaty 8 on behalf of the Chipewyans in the Athabasca region; Chief Martin signed on behalf of the Cree. Discovering that Mom had lost her treaty status when she married Dad, a Métis, frustrated me. I later applied for treaty status under Bill C-31. Mom is also reinstated, and I am second generation to her. Our treaty status ends with me, and is denied to my son because Bill C-31 status is limited to two generations.

Chief Laviolette had heard that the Dominion of Canada had purchased land from Hudson's Bay Company. Aboriginal people's traditional territories became Canada's frontier. As settlers were encouraged to encroach on Native land in the south, reserve lands were allocated to Aboriginal peoples. Chief Laviolette became increasingly concerned that his people would lose their traditional hunting and fishing rights and territory, so he began his campaign to secure reserve land. It took him the better part of three decades before the federal government allocated reserve lands for his people, reserve lands which are today being encroached upon by industry.

Back then, the trappers in the north were dependant on the Hudson's Bay Company trading post in Fort Chipewyan for supplies like guns and food in exchange for their furs, but the trappers were never duly paid in fairness. Though the Hudson's Bay Company thrived as a multimillion dollar business, the Indian and Métis people who assisted in opening the fur trade industry in every capacity are without shares, much as they were when first trading their furs.

During the fur trade era, the first generation of Indian children had begun to be placed in residential schools. A small percentage of these children were orphans as a result of deaths due to diseases, primarily the smallpox epidemic, but the majority were later apprehended as a result of a law passed by the federal government in 1920 that required Indian children to be placed in residential schools. In 1883, residential schools began to be established by churches in cooperation with the government, and by 1920, approximately 130 institutions existed throughout Canada. Indian children then became commodities to churches, worth an average of one hundred dollars per child per year.

The more I learned about our history, the more I saw the not-so-hidden truths of Indigenous people's co-existence with Canada. It left a bitter taste in my mouth, sending me on the warpath for a long time. *She-Greets-with-Fists-First* could have been my name, until all that was left of me was a feeling of victimization as I righteously raged against society and anyone who dared to ridicule *us Indians*.

Then I realized that not everyone was aware of the truth, and some people were generally as uneducated about our history as I once was. I didn't have the right to rip anyone's head off simply because I was carrying a cross, and I couldn't justify my anger and live peacefully with myself, or others.

My life was a double edged sword. In mainstream society, I often felt invaded by people who expected me to provide answers to the plight of Aboriginal issues. How do you bottle in one conversation Canadian and First Nations' history, and make rational sense of something as complex as treaties? If I wasn't being held hostage to intellectual warfare, I was battling stereotypes, and picking up the slack of everyone's romance with Pocahontas. Some people only wanted to hear what they wanted to hear, which was usually diluted with noble notions of being an Indian.

I merely wanted to work and function in life productively, but when I entered the mainstream of Canada I was faced with several controversial enigmas of Aboriginal people. My only consolation was that some people were sincerely interested in learning the truth about our history. There are people interested in learning about our deep roots in Canada, and those who only want to explore cultural activities.

I too had only begun unravelling a tapestry of neatly woven misconceptions hidden within the mosaic of this magnificent country. The faded colours of historical secrets were revealed by the hands of our women who gave birth to a nation and embroidered eloquently upon this blanket. Their blood remains a stain, reminding me of where I come from.

STREET SURVIVORS

Sometimes the only place that felt familiar and, ironically, safe, was the drag. I drove nostalgically through the old neighbourhood, wanting to connect with people who I knew understood what it was like. Whether I was in my car or walking, it was a familiar area of Edmonton for me, and I didn't have to be anyone but myself. I had a kinship with street people. They had no pretence or phoniness; what you saw was what you got, and I respected that.

Most days, my rebellious spirit wanted to ride off on a Harley just to feel free in my skin.

The fact of the matter is, I was born into circumstances out of my control and I grappled with acquiring life skills to live a productive life beyond the streets. Like most people, I want to earn a good living and make the transition into Canadian society, but like several thousand other First Nations and Métis people, I am still discarding generations of residential school syndrome, oppression, abuse and cycles of alcoholism.

Driving downtown, I thought of the twelve-year-old girl I was when I ran away from home, so long ago, and as I reflected on the life of my adopted daughter, I could easily place both of us among the faces of so many young women who are exploited and abused. I've witnessed several reactions to people who live high-risk lifestyles. There is empathy or violent animosity; some people view those who live high-risk lifestyles as a feature of any urban setting, and they couldn't care less. People unfamiliar with the street subculture usually laugh, pointing as though they were at a circus, while others drive by aghast, disgusted. Occasionally, a rare event occurs: People do not see a prostitute, sex trade worker, "ho" and every stereotype that comes with these labels; they see a woman or a man, doing what they have to do to survive.

Imagine the unimaginable when it comes to johns. As with any business, the clientele create revenue. It takes all kinds to keep this business thriving, and the rules are that people provide a service to their clientele through a variety of sexual acts in exchange for money.

In this occupation, women are always at risk of a bad date. Bad dates assume they have the right to be violent, ridicule, demoralize or punish these people, and even kill them. Not *all* people are of the opinion that the life of a person in this business is worthless, but enough condone it, through lack of action and not advocating for the human rights of the people in this business, that acts of violence and murder are perpetuated.

When I see people who live high-risk lifestyles, I am left with an eerie, sad feeling, not because of what they do, and not because of the odds against them in their profession, which is in itself enough to concern me; it's the voices that say, "What do they expect? They put themselves out there, and they get what they deserve." This is by far the scariest rebuttal a human being can make when another human being is found murdered or is missing.

Don't shame my skin. You don't know what my skin has carried me through. What do you see when you look at me, standing cold and alone on the street? Am I a beast in human form in your eyes, with blisters and boils, which are all that remain of what was once purity and innocence, before my skin was peeled by a pedophile's touch, leaving me with scars that remain dormant and deep, from when I was a child. Can you look beyond your fear and animosity to see the one part of me that barely remains alive, yet has endured more than anyone will ever imagine – my spirit? My spirit lives, lonely and scared. What would it take to show you I am a woman, whose womb carried infants, and whose breasts have nurtured their lives as babies? I am a warrior whose plight is survival, and I take courage when walking the streets to sell my body, which was never mine to feel comfortable in. Don't shame my skin – you don't know what my skin has carried me through.

KINDRED SPIRITS

I no sooner turned my head than Matthew was coming home to live with me in grade five. I had long since discovered that being a mom was something I could do, and what I loved more than anything. In keeping with my nomadic nature, I moved Matthew in the middle of his school year, from Edmonton to Saskatoon. He had access to Dan, his stepmom Kate, his stepbrother and stepsister and me all at the same time for the first time since Dan and I had divorced.

I rested comfortably knowing my son was home with me, and together we carried on in our quiet routine. I'd been sober long enough to mature into parenting, although I remained confused in many areas of my life. Of course, there were always relapses into relationships, but for the most part, when Matthew lived with me, relationships were my least concern. I didn't have time to unravel the emotional knots of being involved intimately · with anyone.

Our time together flew by faster than I cared for, and the times of leaving Matthew were the most heart-wrenching moments in my life. Neither of us were ever prepared for parting from each other without deep sadness. It never got any easier, regardless of how often we said good-bye, and as Dan or Kate drove away with Matthew, he would watch me too. I'd drive off into my life without him, filling the void and preoccupying my time with adventures only I, with my flare for the dramatic, could create.

Grade seven with Matthew proved to be an interesting year: I moved five times, through three provinces, and almost lost Matthew during the last move. He informed me that he wanted to live with his dad because he didn't want to move around any-more. I promised to stop moving, and he finished grade seven in Saskatoon. He settled me down. By the end of the year I con-tinued wandering.

Matthew and I maintained our balancing act, and he regis-tered in grade nine in Spruce Grove, travelling back and forth from Edmonton. At the time he started school, I lived in Spruce Grove, and then found a job in Edmonton, and Matthew didn't want to transfer schools midway, so he caught a ride with an acquaintance of mine to Spruce Grove on school days.

I usually picked him up after school, with my music blaring, wearing my black leather jacket and knee-high suede boots. His friends thought I was cool. I was his cheerleading squad at all his volleyball games and tournaments, often screaming advice from the bleachers. "Kick their ass!" abrasively slipped out once, for which he reprimanded me. I promised to contain myself from then on.

Matthew rebelled against my free-spirited gypsy lifestyle over the years, landing firmly on his feet, focusing on his studies and sports. We remained busy, as I thrived on being financially inde-pendent while working as a freelance reporter for Access Television.

Matthew alternated holidays between Dan and me, and this year he was spending Christmas with his dad and stepmom. Most Christmases guarantee a dark cloud looming over me, and this year was no different. I fell into a suicidal depression once Matthew left for the holidays.

Fantasizing about death came naturally. It just hadn't happened in a long time, and thinking about death left me feeling crazy, yet hopeful it would all end. Knowing it was selfish, I stopped asking how I could even think about it. All the common sense, logic and sanity in the world couldn't relieve me of my death wish. I stared at the television, and followed through with scenarios of what would happen. I saw Matthew walking in and finding me dead. I knew I couldn't leave him with that pain. When Matthew was born, he became my only reason to live, but the older he became, the more often my death wish revisited me.

Post-trauma disorder is what my psychologist termed it, as I sat in her chair, trying once again to define the indefinable paradoxes of me. I hadn't been in therapy for several months. She expressed her concerns regarding me missing sessions. Though she was grateful I returned, and chose to live this time. It wasn't the only time I contemplated suicide. In the past, I went to my sessions, until it became too much to handle. Processing the memories of sexual abuse took its toll, and I ran rather than see things through.

There were times I simply wanted to live, be happy and not be consumed with me, me, me and my issues. I didn't know then that I was playing a deadly game. I agreed to continue with therapy, and if I became overwhelmed in our sessions, I would tell her and we would resume when I was ready.

Matthew returned from his holiday, after being away for ten days, and we carried on like nothing had happened.

Three months later, I was working on a special news report when I received a long-distance phone call. Dwayne had died. I went into shock, unable to hold back the scream rising from deep within. "No! What happened? When?" I hung up the phone after Chery gave me all the details.

A co-worker came to my side. In a daze, I walked to the executive producer's office, informing him that I was leaving. There was a death. A colleague offered to drive me home, and as much as Tara wanted to console me, I wouldn't allow her to. I walked away. She ran after me and grabbed my shoulder and spun me around, forcibly holding onto me. I crumbled in Tara's arms, and as my knees buckled, I sobbed.

It was March. Dwayne left us in body but not in spirit. He watches over us and guides us, those he left behind who loved him dearly.

I'm flying lucidly among the stars, mesmerized in adoration of planet Earth. Dwayne's deep monotone voice rises amid the galaxy, where burrowed beyond time, a sorrow and loneliness bursts over and out, as pulsating sobs cave my chest in pain. Dwayne consoles me as I weep, assuring me that he walks among the stars with me, never apart from me. True to his nature, he speaks of the many mysteries of life among the stars, reciting a beautiful poem that he wrote for me.

Early in 1998, I found a job as a client support worker at a resource drop-in centre for the inner-city population of people who live high-risk lifestyles. From 1994 through to 1996, Health Canada funded Kindred House as a pilot project, and then in 1996, the Boyle McCauley Health Centre assumed responsibility. Today, Kindred House is a project sponsored by the Boyle McCauley Health Centre in Edmonton. The doors are open five days a week, for five hours. Kindred House provides human resource services to women who live high-risk lifestyles, advocating on their behalf for additional resources when necessary, and providing much needed stability and consistency to these women.

I'd lost my sense of humour as I struggled through another depression. I didn't like living off welfare or struggling financially while Matthew was with me. It wasn't how I wanted our last year of living together to end. Being employed at Kindred House saved my sanity.

Matthew found part-time work for his spending money, and all he asked of me was to pay the bills and buy food. Taking care of Matthew without concerning him with my mental state as I coped with another depression was my priority. I wanted to provide more than the basics for him, to do different things with him, and at the very least, pay for his extracurricular activities, only to realize that reality fell short of the expectations I placed on myself.

Yet we managed, and the order of our day still began with a hug good morning and ended with another hug good night. Additional hugs in between were permitted at home. Matthew was weaning me off public displays of affection, at least around his friends. This emotional-physical restraining order of adolescence began when he was thirteen, and I still wasn't used to it, although I respected his wishes.

I failed to realize the value of our time together. Depression has a way of blindfolding a person to the benefits of life, and being employed at Kindred House removed the blindfold. The women of Kindred House helped me see the light. I learned to appreciate the basics of living one day at a time and maintaining an attitude of gratitude. They also reminded me of where I had ended up years ago, and that I couldn't walk away from my childhood unscathed or unscarred. It didn't matter where I had come from; what mattered was what was I doing with my life today, and more importantly, what was the quality of my life.

The women of Kindred weren't preached at – that wasn't our role, and it wasn't what they needed. We were there to aid and support them. I'd never encountered a group of people as down-to-earth or ridiculously amusing. Despite themselves and their circumstances, they had a wacky sense of self-ridicule. Though I knew that beneath their laughter were pain, heartache and lost love, these women were real and raw, with personal dreams like anyone else. I found myself entertained while maintaining house regulations: no alcohol, drugs, violence, threats or men, and no one under eighteen.

Each woman reflected a part of me as they recounted their horrific past, placing a shattered mirror in front of my childhood flashbacks. I understood how the blueprints in our lives traced back to sexual abuse, and into a high-risk lifestyle. After each shift, returning to the cosy comforts of my home somehow softened my pillow more and cushioned my heart a whole lot.

I knew that several women of Kindred didn't have a home: they lived on the streets, or had shared accommodations, but wherever they laid their head at night, it likely wasn't safe. I arrived at work most days with enthusiasm, knowing Kindred House provided a safe place for the women to relax, watch movies, or rummage through the used clothes bin after a night of not being safe. Here, they could prepare meals in a kitchen, or have a coffee and smoke cigarettes. Then we would sit around and tell stories, becoming an extended family where no one was judged.

Opening doors in my life had been a long and arduous process as a survivor, so when my shift began with opening the doors of Kindred, I did so with kindness, making coffee, checking messages. Within a half hour, the women began arriving. In between our visiting, I would ensure we had a full inventory of condoms, and, if needed, distributed personal hygiene products, shampoo, toothbrushes and toothpaste, most of which were donated. Before the doors were locked, everyone helped with dishes, and I swept and washed the floors.

Once a week I went to the food bank and picked up a week's supply of groceries. Most volunteers showed up when the doors opened, and a veteran volunteer arrived with home-baked cakes, cookies, and fudge or fresh fruit. The women appreciated her personal touch.

I'd watch the women prepare their personas for the night, while others dropped in to relax and touch base with each other. It was a safe haven for everyone. Our conversations were wild and rambunctious, most of the time, and we had serious tender moments, talking about our children, families and loved ones. The women usually needed a sounding board, and if they wanted my opinion or advice, they asked. I learned not to assume for a second that I could rescue anyone. All that was required of me was unconditional love and acceptance, and good listening skills.

We talked about life, health, love and financial struggles, and anything that had happened since we'd last gathered around the kitchen table. We enjoyed a game of outwitting one another, to see who could come up with the most shockingly crude comments or anecdotes. I held my own, much to everyone's delight. There wasn't much they could say to faze me. Our twisted humour was at the expense of ourselves, not anyone else.

I grew to love all of the women of Kindred. I appreciated their hugs and enthusiasm after not seeing each other for more than a few days, enjoying some of the women who made spectacular entrances. Together, it was hard to be depressed, or down and out; someone always rallied around anyone having a hard time. The camaraderie was uplifting, and even I couldn't remain depressed before someone would ask if I was okay and if need be, call me on my attitude.

Meanwhile, the more inexperienced virginal volunteers were easy game for women who had their own methods of shock therapy. They thrived on making people squirm, while I sat back in mixed amusement and empathy as a volunteer was being initiated. Most returned. The few volunteers who didn't, shouldn't have. Initiating volunteers allowed the women to see who could handle it and who couldn't. A person had to be able to see beyond human frailties caused by a harsh life to view these women as people. How could they respect or care for the women if they were hung up on façades or fear? The women weren't abusive, nor did they cross the line. Volunteers either became nervous and embarrassed, or jumped in like a dirty old T-shirt in good humour.

There is nothing romantic about prostitution, or the lifestyle. *Pretty Woman* it isn't, and being rescued by a millionaire couldn't be further from the reality these women live. Many worked for the next fix, and whether through a needle or a "date," their risk of contracting STDs, hepatitis or AIDS was substantial. Not all women who live high-risk lifestyles are addicts, and they all work to feed themselves, and for many, their children.

It isn't the street subculture that presents danger; the threat lies within a percentage of people who venture onto the streets preying on people who live high-risk lifestyles. These predators bring their malice and evil intent into the street subculture. The street population takes care of each other, and where humanity often hides its face in mainstream society, you can recognize humanity here. Every day, small acts of love can save a life. Sharing food, shelter, blankets to stay warm, a kind word or listening to a person makes a difference. The offering of a cigarette or food goes a long way. Loving thy neighbour isn't laborious; it's their code of survival, and your neighbour is a brother or sister.

All of the women cared for each other, and when someone new showed up on the drag or at Kindred House, they were welcomed, and the regulars warned them of who to watch out for, making sure the new person was equipped to survive.

At Kindred House we had what was known as the blue code. This code means an attempt has been made on the life of one of the women. In the event of a blue code, the women receive a description of the assailant, the vehicle, and the circumstances involved in the assault. This kind of information could save someone's life, something Kindred House tried to do on a daily basis, in more ways than one. While I worked at Kindred House, rumours of a serial killer were rampant in Vancouver, and everyone was aware of the eerie numbers of missing women. This caused more sadness than anxiety amongst our clients because several of the women of Kindred knew some of the missing women personally.

EMPTY NEST

Working part time at Kindred provided me with a minimal fixed income, which I subsidized with welfare, yet I was only too happy to be working, even though I had no money for extras. We had food and a roof over our heads. My perspective on life had changed since coming to Kindred. I saw the value of what we had, instead of focusing on what we didn't. Matthew continued to thrive in school while he worked part time bussing tables in a restaurant, which provided him with enough money to travel with his team to tournaments.

By May, we had moved into a two-bedroom house near Clarke Stadium, close to the ravine. The owners, an elderly retired couple, lived next door, and they helped Matthew and me plant a garden. It was my first garden, and I discovered I had a natural green thumb as I ploughed the earth, planted seeds and watched buds blossom through spring. I spent a lot of time in my garden enjoying my new hobby, and by early summer we had a variety of fresh vegetables to choose from.

The ravine trails began at our back alley, where there were no houses to block the view of trees in the river valley. I jogged daily, or worked out at Clarke Stadium with Matthew, when he had time.

Matthew's final year of living with me haunted me like a shadow, and I found myself pushing him away emotionally in an effort to lessen the blow of letting go, which only hurt him as I selfishly battled with my fears of abandonment. When Matthew left, I realized how I had subconsciously pushed him away since he was fourteen, leaving me remorseful as I anguished over how hard he had struggled to remain part of my life, despite my often abusive behaviour.

I was visiting a friend on the Blood reserve after Matthew moved back with Dan for grade twelve. Early in the morning, I took a walk, admiring the monumental presence of the mountains while filled with grief over my empty nest. I didn't know what to do with my life. Up until then, Matthew had been my central station, and my destinations revolved around him. I spoke with my grandmothers, asking for guidance and understanding, and then I had a moment of clarity.

I remembered a simple little prayer I had said several years past: "God, I don't want to die. I need to watch my son become a man." I had asked to live, to watch Matthew become a man. Now Matthew was a man, and somewhere deeply embedded in my psyche was the belief that my life, my reason for living, was now over. I realized that I had to live my life fully, and let go of Matthew, so he could live his life.

I decided to move out of Edmonton, and sadly parted from the women of Kindred House. I'd been contemplating what I wanted to do after Matthew moved when, thankfully, my friend Hazel invited me to live with her in Alberta Beach.

Hazel lived in a house on the shore of Lac Ste. Anne with her son and daughter, and now me. My stay with her family involved a wonderful fictitious world of waiting for UFOs and hoping for contact from the mother ship. Hazel had managed to convince the townsfolk that UFOs existed. She took pleasure in converting the most rigid sceptics, who found themselves watching for UFOs when no one was watching them.

Hazel and I spent coffee hours in her kitchen, on her deck, or warmly wrapped in blankets beneath the stars on cool nights. We talked esoterically about every imaginable phenomenon, and the greatest phenomenon yet, relationships, and our inability to function sanely in them.

Sleeping came easy for me in her house near the shore, as the lake's lullaby allowed my dreams to effortlessly sail into the night.

My sheer white chiffon scuffles over dirt as I traipse along a trail, running past evening shadows, wildly searching for a man whose act of kindness upon me, a scorned wench, moved me to tears. He witnessed my soul, and saw beyond my adulteress's sins, invoking self-forgiveness before he vanished.

I run into the night, desperate to find him, needing to thank him. Mary Magdalene greets me near an ancient cobblestone gate, extending her hand, asking why the hurry and distress. I plead with her, "Please help me find this man." She motions for me to follow her.

I balk as we come upon a bridge crossing a mile-wide river. I hear moans rising from the river and as I look down, I see hundreds upon hundreds of decaying women who scream, wail and mourn among themselves. Suspended in self-condemnation, I ask Mary where we are. "This is the river of wailing women," she tells me. "These women choose to remain in the river of their own accord. Each one has free will to walk away, yet many remain throughout the ages, surrendering to their own grief."

We pass over the bridge and come upon a hill where a majestic cathedral towers above. Mary points toward a trail, instructing me to follow it to the cathedral, then vanishes. In the cathedral, I pass several people I'd known before, all of whom are preoccupied with their lives and unable to see me. A monk directs me toward a spiral staircase leading to the tower.

Within the tower, a nun stops me from opening a door. I plead with her to tell the man I am waiting. She won't permit me to see him, fearing I will attempt to seduce him.

I begg her to allow me in. She still refuses to open the door, and then suddenly the man stands before me, blinding me with his brilliant presence. I fall to my knees as the voice of God proclaims, "The angels of heaven herald in glory as one act of kindness is bestowed on Earth, for an act of love is greater than all the worldly deeds known to man."

Humbled, I tremble in his merciful presence, as an aura of radiating light extends onto me, blessing me.

That morning, I strolled along the beach. The sun was hot as I sat on a log, reflecting on the precious time I had had to watch Matthew become a young man. Our time together came and went as swiftly as the waves that touched the shore and were whisked away.

The summer months I shared with Hazel also came to an end, and I wandered on with my life. My gypsy spirit eventually brought me to Isabelle's home in Merritt, British Columbia. Isabelle is a bear woman, and her lodge was a sage den and safe refuge during several of my attempts to salvage what little sanity I could. Through the years, I have crawled into her cave a destitute woman, and over time, I came to understand that the spirits chased me to her doorstep. The grandmothers knew her hearth was my only hope because Isabelle understood the spirits. She could hear them, feel them, and smell them. She understood how fragile the link between spirit world and reality is. And in Isabelle's house, spirits and people who felt crazy like me were welcomed.

Isabelle's brown eyes remained kind and compassionate while I raged and ranted, and her voluptuous body moved like the she-bear she is, with deliberate and patient intent. Isabelle is a strong woman, and someone I trust. Being a strong woman too, when I met Isabelle, I appreciated her stealth, and how she walked in her power with kindness, with wounds that softened her heart rather than hardened it. I needed to learn how to be kind, while she needed to be reminded that it's okay to roar if she had to. We were a bear and a lone wolf who happened to cross paths, to share the secrets of our sacred ground.

Sometimes the grandmothers can drag a good woman through mud and sticks and over sharp rocks that cut deeply, just to teach a lesson. And if you're stubborn, the willows are brought out. More times than not, I arrived at Isabelle's licking my wounds because of my stubbornness. Isabelle always laughed at me, and then tended my wounds with her mud medicine, enough for the bleeding to stop and the healing to begin. Isabelle knew a little pain never hurt anyone, and the grandmothers' pain always had a point. She also knew better than to interfere with spirits or what the spirits willed.

And always, Isabelle and I threw the riddles of our lives on the table to sort through during our soul-searching conversations, and amid his pile I had an epiphany one day. "I understand what the dream meant." She watched me curiously. "I have to make an offering to his spirit and forgive him so he can move on." She nodded in agreement. I didn't have to elaborate. I appreciated that about her: I never had to explain myself. I'd met Isabelle several years past, and ever since, we'd nurtured our eccentricities and commonalities, weeding our girlfriend garden with mutual love and respect.

Our council was created innocently enough, one evening as we methodically lit our cigarettes, puffing smoke intently as our issues smouldered into ashes. My medicine bag of hot air released spirits that mourned to tell stories of broken beer promises, and honeymoon hickey lovers who waltzed into my heart, and left. I entertained Isabelle many nights with my many trails of broken hearts. We often contemplated our sanity; which led to bitching; this stirred anger, churning the decay of sexual abuse and depression that matted years of emotions into a gargoyle mask of self-deception.

There was a time when I didn't know what depression was – being lethargic, moody or hypersensitive was the norm. I eventually made peace with my internal clock and chaotic hormones enough to rest when depressed, permitting my spirit to wander within dream trance, giving my soul a reprieve and my mind a rest. Sleep loosens the knot in the noose. I slip into an ethereal state of deep unconsciousness, a safe place, where I visit the spirit world. In the *real* world, I was once led to believe that I was insane, so I appreciate the psychosis of my dreams, most of the time.

Blood is crawling into the cracks of the wood floor and I'm acutely aware of the knife in his hand. His precision is an art as he slices flesh, gingerly peeling fat and muscle away from the carcass. I search his eyes, yet he ignores me. He is fixated on his kill. His expression is calm and he is mute. Dark, dull eyes mesmerize me, along with the movement of his saturated bloody hands. Dry blood covered with fresh blood, creating a second skin. I watch carefully. The cabin is empty except for us, and I'm curious about why we're in the cabin because I know he's dead. He's been dead for a long time. Suddenly my mom is standing beside me. She motions me to be quiet. I whisper, "Why is he here?" She gives me a stern look, warning me. I realize we're in a sacred place. He finishes skinning the moose; now he is cutting the hind, ribs and head off. I understand I'm allowed to watch in silence, and I'm not afraid.

Later, I prepared a humble feast, lit my sage and sweetgrass, and smudged myself and my offerings. I prayed and set a plate for Jake. We talked for a long time, Jake and me. I then placed his offerings outside. I asked him to carry on in his spirit journey. "I forgive you," I said. Then I watched Jake's spirit turn away from me. He disappeared into the spirit world. He was at peace. Jake hasn't returned in my dreams since. He went home.

BEAR-WALKER THE MAN

Matthew was ten years old when he received his spirit name, Bear-Walker, and I received my name, Morning-star. I was dancing at a Sun Dance when we were given our names. I hadn't asked to be named, so when I was told, I was humbled. Who am I to question the grandmothers, or the Great Mystery's will for me?

The year before I had received this name, I once again struggled with depression, only this time, it was more of a grieving process than anything. I couldn't understand what was happening with me, when one night a friend arrived at my door at two in the morning. He told me he didn't know why he was there other than that he needed to know if I was okay. I said, "No I'm not okay. Take me out of the city. I need to make an offering."

We drove outside of the city and found a quiet place. I asked to be alone and walked away. I made an offering of tobacco and became overwhelmed with grief so intense that my body convulsed with sobs. I found myself screaming into the universe, "Jolene, don't leave me, I'm not ready to let you go." I didn't know then that I was grieving the loss of my old self. I received my name, Morningstar, the following summer.

For three months after I was given my name, when anyone spoke it, I felt a tingling sensation throughout my body, as though I were waking, until one day I woke completely conscious of myself and grounded in my skin, centered.

I resumed life with a quiet sense of self.

Years later, Matthew's honour roll status won him several awards and scholarships, throughout high school and into university. When he was eighteen, in his first year of mechanical engineering, he invited me to an awards ceremony in Regina where he received another scholarship. I wasn't prepared for what would happen, and I attempted to deal with this milestone moment in our relationship as mother and son as honestly and gracefully as I could.

We were having breakfast when Matthew allowed himself to express his pain and anger toward me. I had always encouraged him to be honest with me, and he decided to exercise his prerogative that day. Matthew cried as he spoke of his anger and the resentment he had harboured over the years for having been abandoned and rejected by me since he was a baby, and how this theme continued all his life. He referred to the cruelty of my pushing him away from me, emotionally and psychologically.

When he finished, Matthew sat across from me, emotionally spent, his eyes reddened from crying. I waited for him to calm. I took a deep breath, and admitted to everything he had said. I owned up to rejecting and abandoning him when he was a baby, and freely acknowledged how I had treated him later in life. Not once did I attempt to justify my behaviour or deny anything. It was the truth and it all had to be expressed, there was no doubt in my mind about that.

I offered him the option of not having anything to do with me again, and I would respect his decision and not contact him until he felt comfortable enough to contact me first. But if he decided to remain in my life, it would be with the understanding that we would work through our pain and any issues between us. We left it at that. I said I'd wait to hear from him, and that I loved him with all my heart.

We hugged goodbye, and I drove back to Alberta a wreck, yet relieved that Matthew had spoken of what he had obviously struggled with. Knowing how long he had carried his pain, and that he had finally placed it where it belonged – with me – made me feel better. I cried too, wondering if and when I would hear from him. I was only too willing to assume responsibility for my behaviour, and how my actions had hurt him. All I could do was wait, and pray; he would decide to do what was best for himself.

I was willing to accept any decision he made regarding whether I could remain in his life. As much as the idea of not being part of his life hurt, I surrendered, as I had when he was five years old, when he decided to move back with his dad.

Three months later, he phoned me. He asked how I was, letting me know he was doing well, and that he had had time to think things through. And when the time was right, he would share his thoughts with me. In the meantime, he missed me, and yes, he wanted me in his life.

Matthew could have easily moved on with his life without me, and I wouldn't have blamed him. I understood his need to create boundaries with me, through my own need to create boundaries with my mom because of our challenging relationship.

I moved on with my life without a road map or destination, my bags packed and my Indian car still intact and ready to go. I travelled around, visiting, spending much of my time living with Isabelle and her husband. Within one year, I wandered through Merritt, Edmonton, Vancouver, Saskatoon and Ottawa, attend another awards ceremony for Matthew, and then flew to New York. I sustained my free-spirited flight, landing on the shores of Lake Athabasca, going home to Fort Chipewyan after twenty years.

The highlight of being home was touching base with several people I hadn't seen in over twenty years, especially the old-young-timers at the lodge, who invited me to join their morning coffee breaks. It was the one boys' club I didn't mind infiltrating. They told stories of days gone by in good old oral fashion. I took time out to visit my favourite places of reclamation, strolling along the shore of Lake Athabasca, listening to the familiar clanging of a steel ball weight that chimed against a flag-pole, rhythmically echoing for miles. Dogs barked in the distance, and the occasional vehicle rumbled over pavement, which was new to me. The town had paved the dirt roads, which are now black asphalt, all the way from the airport to Dog Head, where I climbed a hill and escaped into Mother Earth's womb.

Quiet ceremony, miles of silence fossilize my grandmothers' and grandfathers' footprints pounded into the land. Their voices are into-nations of Nature's music mulching muskeg, moss and dried cran-berry leaves over moccasin foot trails. Stirring awake organic burial grounds, evoking ancestral drum songs, whose language is earth-wind-rock-water tones as I walk the earth on the bones of my ances-tors, whose spirits smudge me with sweetgrass and fungus, strengthening me.

From atop the hill, I viewed miles and miles of dense bush, comparing the moment to being amid millions of people in con-stant motion in Manhattan, the city that never sleeps, to a place where time stands still. Sitting on my rock chair, I felt grounded in my skin, so unlike the portraits of Indians I admired while touring the National Museum of the American Indian in Manhattan, where The Canadian Museum of Civilization had held a travelling exhibition, *Reservation X.* This exhibit, filled with a multitude of moccasins, caught my breath as I uncon-sciously shed tears of awe, marvelling over three round glass exhibits that displayed a hand drum in the centre of numerous moccasins. The materials of the moccasins varied. The majority were tanned hides, one pair was of woven grass, another leather sandals. Most were adorned in colourful floral or geometric bead-work, or embroidered with dyed porcupine quills, each pair distinctly authentic to the origin of the Indigenous peoples who designed them. All of the moccasins were worn at some point in history. I tried to imagine the lives of the ancestors who had walked in these moccasins. I couldn't fathom their trails. A simple pair of moccasins carried history, and the variety and distinction of each pair reflected hundreds of Indigenous peoples who once walked Turtle Island.

In my rock chair, on the hill in Fort Chip, I was grateful I could listen to our storytellers. The old-young-timers spoke to me of a time we used dog teams to travel to the drum dances, where the people gathered from far distances, as families left their traplines to return to Fort Chipewyan, trading their furs and restocking dry goods, food and ammunition with the Hudson's Bay. When all the business was taken care of, the people danced for days at a time, well into the night while visiting, feasting and exchanging stories and politics from the winter.

It was the common sense of the stories and the storytellers that entertained me. They had a way of simplifying things in life, to the bare bones of the matter, reminding me of one young man who told me, "People stay here to become good storytellers."

My brief interlude at home rejuvenated me, inspiring me to move on in life. I eventually moved to Calgary and went back to school. I sought another psychologist: I was once again willing to delve into my core issues, and through the guidance and compassion of my psychologist, Margaret, came into myself.

On Matthew's twenty-first birthday, I was a struggling student, so all I could offer my son was a raincheck. I phoned him and asked what he wanted for his birthday. He replied, "Mom, I want you to do whatever you're doing, to the best of your ability, no matter what it is. I don't want you to allow people, places or things to interfere with the goals you set for yourself this year, whether that's studying or working. I believe in you, and I know how much potential you have because I've witnessed it. And your potential is what I want you to focus on this year. I have faith in you, Mom, and whatever you set your mind on, so whenever you feel depressed, or down, think of the gift, and don't give up on yourself. That's what I want for my birthday, and next year at this time, you can tell me what you've accomplished by not giving up on yourself."

I was talking to him at a pay phone, and as he spoke to me, I was brought to my knees as I cried. His ingenious mind caught me, and, once again, he asked me to be accountable and responsible for my attitude and my behaviour.

To fulfil his request, I reflected on all areas of my life, especially therapy. Margaret's methods of healing were as liberating as her philosophy, and I knew we were meant to meet when she asked if I had a concept of a higher power. I did. It was important for her to know I could call upon my grandmothers for strength and courage as we ventured into my pain and past.

Margaret helped me appreciate how deeply embedded points of trauma are encapsulated in my body, and through bodywork we released traumatic memory. It sounded easy enough, but I had no idea how difficult it would be. The benefits of working through the trauma were profoundly healing, and we were able to begin a journey that would catapult me into a sense of self I never had before.

Matthew eventually found the right time to tell me what he had pondered over the three months he hadn't contacted me. He said to me, "Mom, I realize I wouldn't be who I am today if not for you and Dad. I thought about what would have happened if you hadn't sobered up, or if you had abandoned me completely. I know my life wouldn't have been as fulfilling, and I wouldn't have learned the lessons I have. So you see, I'm grateful you're in my life, and I love you because you're my mom, and I'm a better person because of that. It could have been worse, and it is what it is, and we have today."

I realized that I too wouldn't be who I am had it not been for my mom. Her influence on me and my life carried me through similar cycles of abusive patterns and instability, and for many years I felt displaced. But I know one thing: I am a survivor, as is she, and we're both doing the best we can with what we have. I watched her being abused all her life, not knowing anything else, until abuse was the norm. Later in her life, I continued to watch her suffer. Her health slowly deteriorated because of her alcoholism, and only now, I see the woman I've always loved. She is my mom, and I love her for who she is. She is a beautiful person.

My son is the second generation of children who have not been placed in residential schools, and our wounds are mending, for Mom, me and my son. I was a sexually exploited child. Though I have an understanding of who I am today, I know I did what I had to do to survive. I ended up living a high-risk lifestyle, and it could have cost me my life, until one day, one man reminded me that someone cared, if only I would too.

You see, sometimes all it takes is one person to make a difference. One person to tell you everything is going to be all right when your whole world is falling apart and there seems to be no hope.

All I needed was a reason to live. My son is that reason. Eventually, I had to let him go and allow him to live his own life. By then, I knew I could live mine, but not without the care and compassion of countless people who cared for me and loved me when I couldn't love myself. I could have been one of those women who were murdered on the street, but someone cared and I made a choice to live.

I hadn't been employed at Kindred House for more then three years when the discovery of the gruesome murders of women was revealed at the Pickton farm. When I heard the news, I was devastated. My heart ached with the possibility that any one of the women from Kindred House could be among these women.

It would be two years before I would return to Kindred House. In 2003, I briefly visited everyone over Christmas. Only now, there was another series of murders under investigation in Edmonton. Several women overdosed because of the horror and grief of these insidious murders of women who lived high-risk lifestyles.

This epidemic killing spree in Canada leaves hundreds of families in mourning.

In the summer of 2003, I sat in my uncle's living room and watched the local news. What I heard shocked and triggered me. A twelve-year-old Cree girl had been raped by three men in their twenties. Her case was brought to court two years later, and the verdict freed two of the men and placed one man under house arrest while he did community service.

The verdict was a blow that I could not believe. The jury listened to the defendants' lawyers speak of how the girl was the sexual aggressor because she was presumably sexually abused at home. Her history and, consequentially, her behaviour was in question, not the rape. I knew that if she were not Native, the men would not have been freed, and the verdict and punishment would have been far more severe.

WARRIOR WOMEN

To the ones who are strong enough to dance with and slay their demons, to the ones who are slain by their demons, and to the ones carried away by their demons to live in the hell they have created for themselves, aimlessly lost in shame and cycles. To those whose eyes have been gouged from their heads and whose tongues have been cut so the truth cannot be spoken and reality unseen. We, the Warriors, will tell our truth and own it. So don't cry little sisters, and if you do, it's not in vain. We, the Warriors, hear your cries, because we have listened to our own, and have given them a voice.

ACKNOWLEDGEMENTS

My son, Matthew John Dunn – Bear Walker, you are my greatest joy. I love you with my heart and soul. David W. Dunn, Cec, Sean and Tara, John and Sylvia and family, thank you for being who you are to Matthew.

To all six of my beautiful sisters, I love you. To my parents, who survived in silence the Holy Angels Mission, I love you both.

There are people who will remain with you for life, while others are there only for a brief time. I've been blessed to have prayed with many in sweats, feasted and drank tons of coffee with most, and we came to know one another in a good way through laughter and stories. I'm grateful for your influence and friendship: Chief Leonard George, Francoise and Leslie Paulette, Richard Van Camp, Thomas King, Oppie Oppenheim, Richard Wagamese, Brian Maracle, Gary Farmer, Eskimo Fred, Raven and Rita Makinaw, Lone Walker, Warren Goulding, Toby C. Te Aturangi, Murray Townsend, Leona Tootoosis, Mishi, Maria Campbell, Roxanne, Tanis, Cindy, Emma and Louie Cardinal, Maggie Hodgson, Cheryl and Ken, Brenda and Rob Gilchrist, Joyce Tuccaro, Claudia Simpson, Jackie McDermott – Rainbow Woman, Sherie, Lorie-Lei, Miss Jody, Carmen Rose, Louise

Halfe, Hazel Bjourson, Rose Ross, Marlene Chapman, Victoria, Cleo, Nitanis, Honey, Skeena, Cheeko, Nancy, Dee-Dee, Joe, Dr. Louise Million, Dr. Margaret McLeod, Kate Quinn, Julie Zettle – Yellow Thunderbird Woman, Kathy Hamlin, Muriel Stanley Venne, the late Eddie Bellerose, the late Dr. Anne Anderson, the late Clay Bertlemann, the late Chief Dan George. To my editor, Roberta Mitchell Coulter, thank you for your keen eye and patience. There are countless others who have inspired me – thank you for your kindness and caring.

Beth Cuthand and Gerry William, your belief in me and your unconditional love carried me through more than you know. Thank you. The people who matter most keep life in perspective.

ABOUT THE AUTHOR

Morningstar Mercredi is a storyteller, actress, social activist, poet, playwright, researcher and multi-media communicator. She has previously published one non-fiction children's book, *Fort Chipewayan Homecoming*, which was a finalist in the Silver Birch young reader's choice award in Ontario. She has also had poetry published in the *Gatherings* Anthology series. She has done extensive acting work in film, television, radio and on the stage.

Born in Uranium City, Saskatchewan, Morningstar Mercredi has lived in Alberta – Fort Chipewayan, Calgary, and Fort McMurray; Saskatchewan – Saskatoon and Prince Albert; British Columbia – Cranbrook, Kimberly, Merritt, Penticton and Surrey; and the Northwest Territories – Yellowknife and Rae/Edze. She also settled for a time in Gisborne, New Zealand and Nowra, Australia. She currently makes Edmonton her home.

Marquis Book Printing Inc.

Québec, Canada
2008